18 HAPPENINGS
IN SIX PARTS
BY ALLAN KAPROW

THE REUBEN GALLERY
61 4th AVE., N.Y.C.
OCT. 4,6,7,8,9,10--8:30 p.m.

CAST OF PARTICIPANTS

Allan Kaprow - who speaks and plays a musical instrument

Rosalyn Montague - who speaks and moves

Shirley Prendergast - who moves and plays a musical instrument

Lucas Samaras - who speaks, plays a game and a musical instrument

Janet Weinberger - who moves and plays a musical instrument

Robert Whitman - who moves, speaks and plays a game

Sam Francis, Red Grooms, Dick Higgins, Lester Johnson, Alfred Leslie, Jay Milder, George Segal, Robert Thompson - each of whom paints

The visitors - who sit in various chairs

INSTRUCTIONS

The performance is divided into six parts. Each part contains three happenings which occur at once. The beginning and end of each will be signalled by a bell. At the end of the performance two strokes of the bell will be heard.

You have been given three cards. Be seated as they instruct you. That is, be sure to change your place for set three and for set five.

Between part one and part two there is a two minute interval. Remain seated.

Between part two and part three there is a fifteen minute interval. You may move about freely.

Between part three and part four there is a two minute interval when you will remain in your seats.

Between part four and part five there is a fifteen minute interval. You may move about.

Between part five and part six there is a two minute interval. Remain seated.

There will be no applause after each set. You may applaud after the sixth set if you wish, although there will be no "curtain call".

The visitors are please asked not to smoke at all in the loft. They are also asked not to leave the building during the longer intermissions.

Room 1 Set 1

Person 1

All movements will be made according to the cardinal axes ↕↔

walks slowly along corridor (ahead of those going to Room 2), stops at entrance 5", walks slowly in a straight line, eyes ahead, to within 3 feet of the person seated [illegible] opposite, stops here for 7" turns around for 2"; takes one step to the left and proceeds as follows:

① 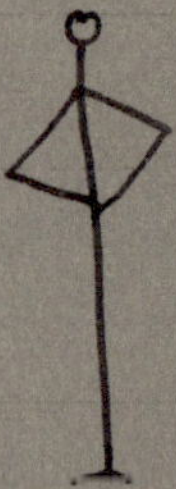

hands on hips

16"

② (side view)

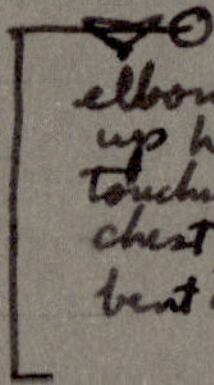

elbows up hands touching on chest, waist bent at angle

5"

③ (side view)

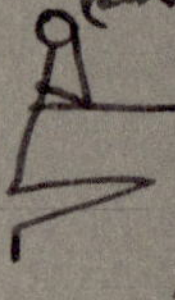

squat knees together one hand raised to forehead, other extended front. All lines perpendicular to floor or parallel

8"

④ 

straight up and down

20"

⑤ turn around on spot quickly

1"

⑥ turn back again quickly

1"

⑦ (side view)

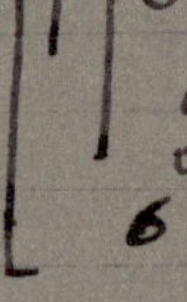

one arm up, one down

6"

Room 1 Set 1

Person 1

(8) (side view)

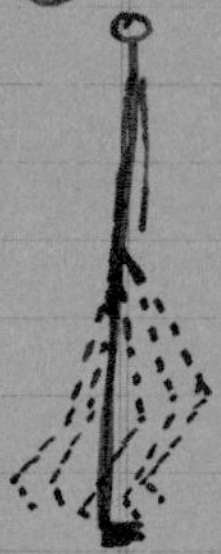

turn right swing left foot slowly back and forth not too far either way

17"

(9) take 22 steps in any cardinal direction changing as often as you wish. Each turn should be made after a near stop and should be a clean angle. Stop. (approx. 22")

(10)

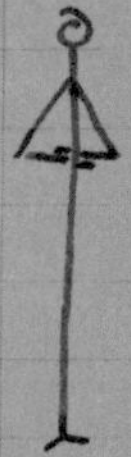

hands clasped behind back, not touching back tho

2"

(11) (side view)

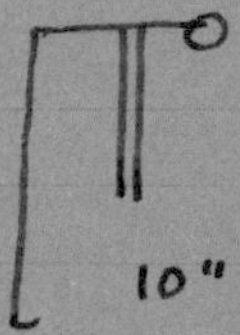

bend over arms hanging straight

10"

(12)

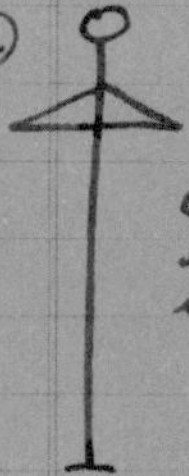

hands on chest, elbows up

12"

(13) two steps forward

2"

(14) (side view)

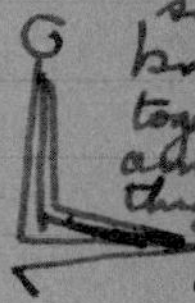

squat, knees together, arms on thighs.

4"

(15) (side view)

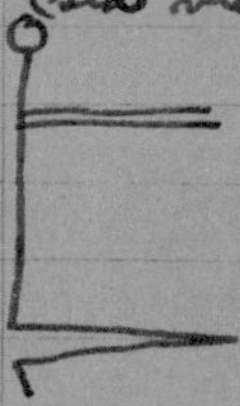

arms extended

1"

(16)

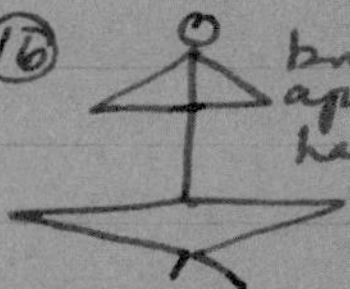

knees apart, hands on chest

2"

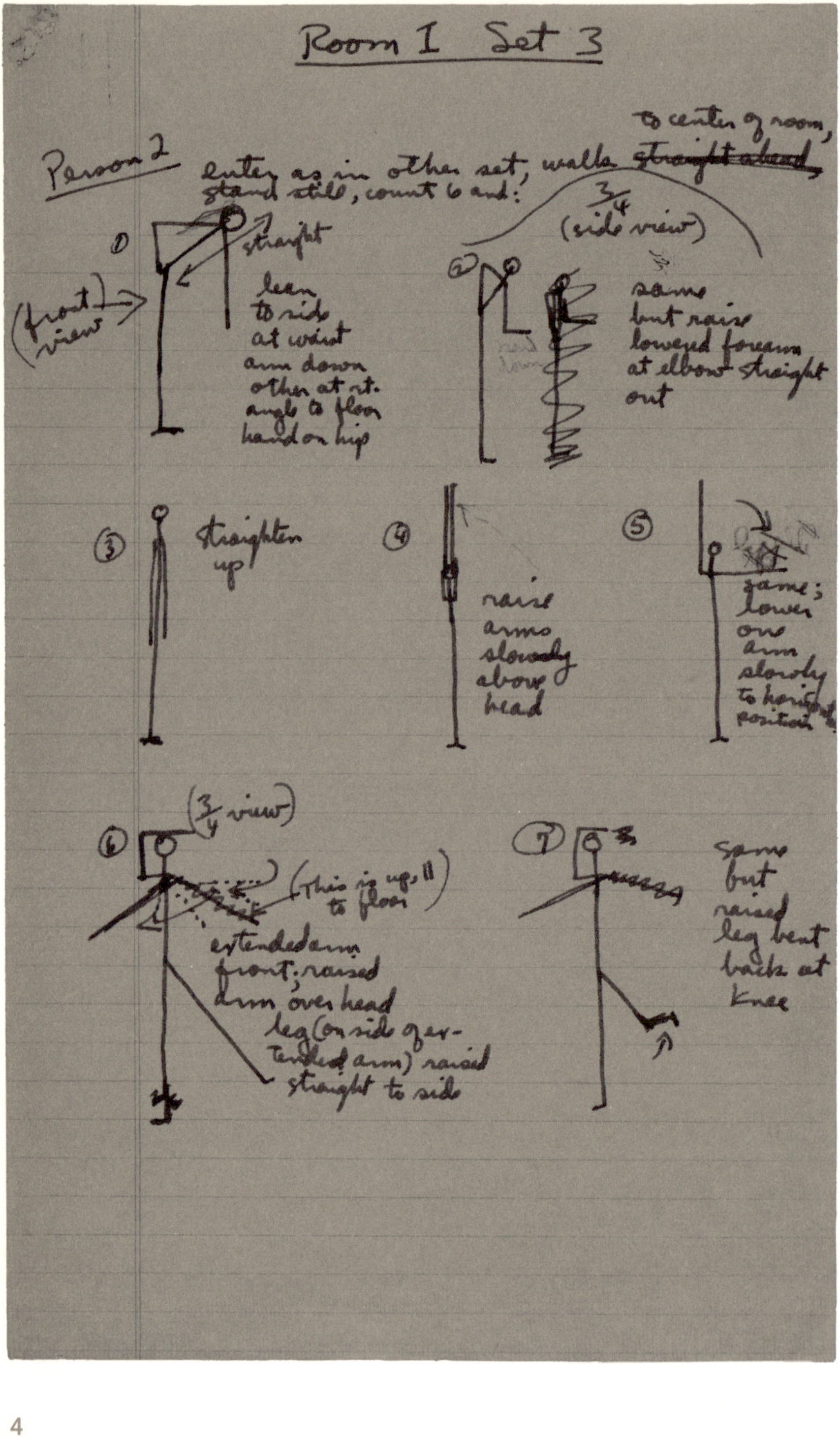

Room I Set 3

Person 2 enter as in other set, walk ~~straight ahead~~ to center of room, stand still, count 6 and:

① (front view) straight — lean to side at waist arm down other at rt. angle to floor hand on hip

3/4 (side view)

② same but raise lowered forearm at elbow straight out

③ straighten up

④ raise arms slowly above head

⑤ same; lower one arm slowly to horizontal position

⑥ (3/4 view) (this is up, ∥ to floor) extended arm front; raised arm over head leg (on side of extended arm) raised straight to side

⑦ same but raised leg bent back at knee

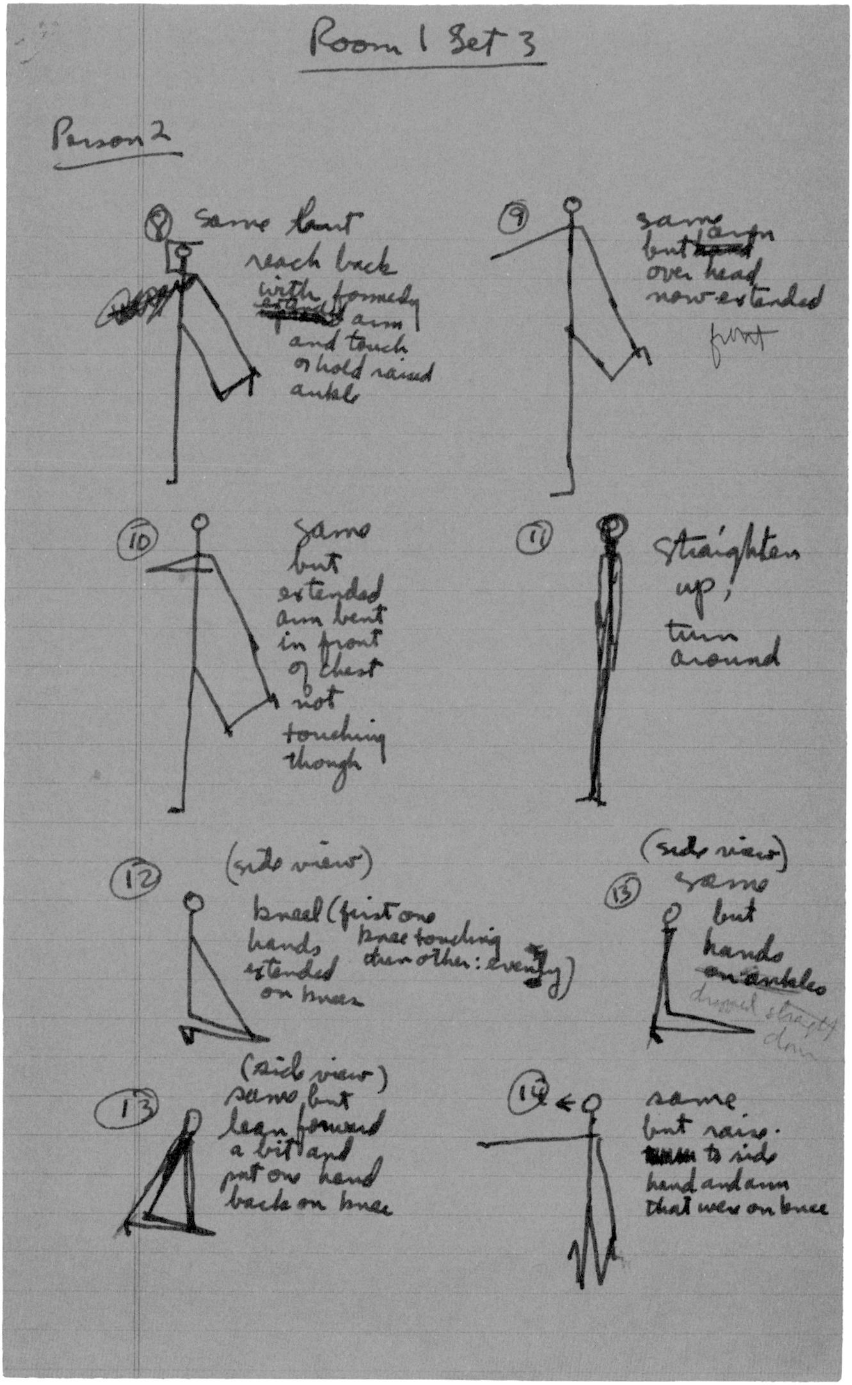

Room 1 Set 3

Person 2

(8) same but reach back with formerly raised arm and touch or hold raised ankle

(9) same but arm over head now extended front

(10) same but extended arm bent in front of chest not touching though

(11) straighten up; turn around

(12) (side view) kneel (first one knee touching then other: evenly) hands extended on knees

(13) (side view) same but hands ~~on ankles~~ dropped straight down

(13) (side view) same but lean forward a bit and put one hand back on knee

(14) ← same but raise to side hand and arm that were on knee

Room 2 Set 1

Person 3

walks down corridor slowly 4" after person 2 does same. Stands at entrance for 1", walks more rapidly than person 2 (but not too rapidly) eyes ahead to end of aisle, turns left, walks to left center (turns to face audience) of room (near left wall), stops 5" (all actions henceforth are arranged according to cardinal directions ✥), arranges arms and legs as follows:

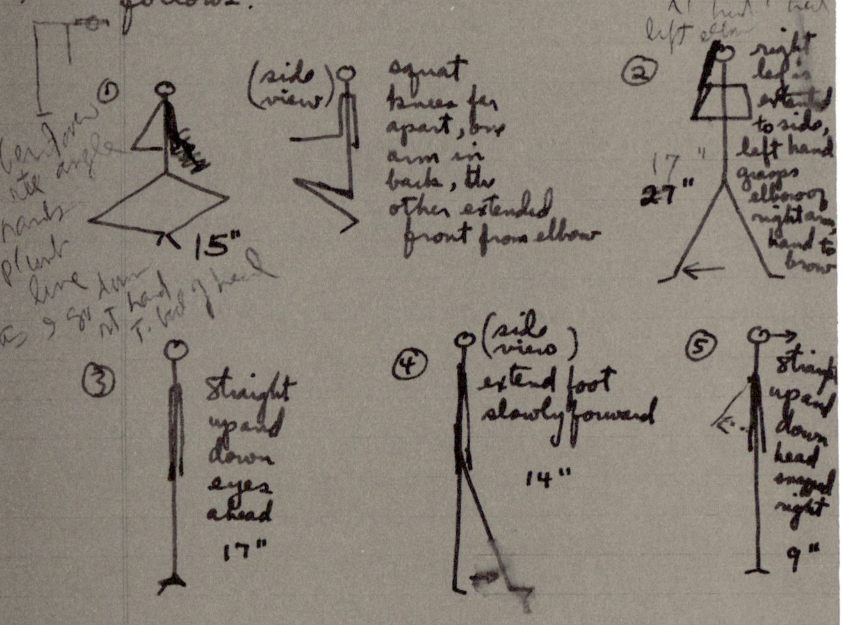

Room 2 Set 1

Person 3

⑥ 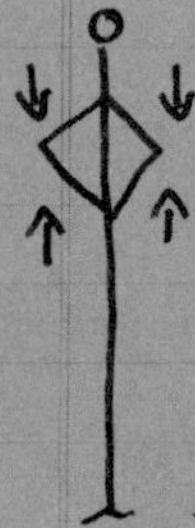

hands on hips slide both hands along sides stopping each time hands are returned to first position

39"

⑦ 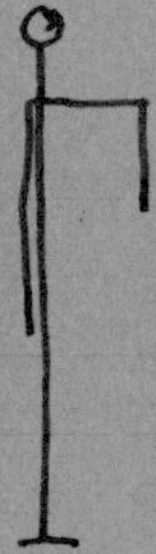

forearm down palm back

10"

⑧ 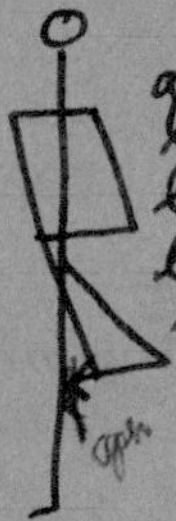

grasp right leg with left hand slowly. Right hand holds left arm at arm crook. Hold

15"

⑨ 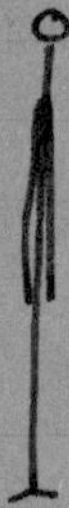

straight up and down eyes left smile after count of 11"

13"

⑩ 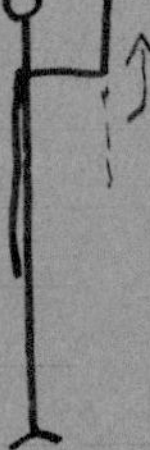

arm up palm ~~back~~ front

21"

⑪ 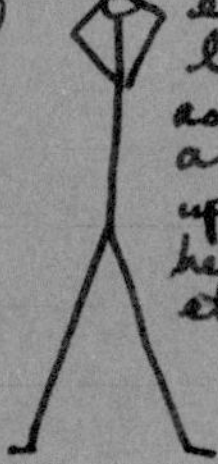

extend left leg - as arms are brought up, hands on head. ~~Snap elbows forward~~

8"

18/6

ALLAN KAPROW 18 HAPPEN-INGS IN 6 PARTS

1–7
——— 18 HAPPENINGS IN 6 PARTS, 1959
Excerpt from the score by Allan Kaprow

13
——— 18 HAPPENINGS IN 6 PARTS
9/10/11 November 2006, Haus der Kunst, Munich, 8:30 pm

45
——— REDOING 18 HAPPENINGS IN 6 PARTS
André Lepecki

53
——— ART AS LIFE
KUNST ALS LEBEN
Haus der Kunst, Munich, October 2006–January 2007
KUNST ALS LEVEN
Van Abbemuseum, Eindhoven, Feburary–April 2007

69
——— MUSEUM AS MEDIATION
Eva Meyer-Hermann

73
——— THE RISK OF WELCOMING THE PUBLIC
Stephanie Rosenthal

79
——— BIOGRAPHY

80
——— COLOPHON

18 HAPPENINGS IN 6 PARTS BY ALLAN KAPROW

9/10/11 November 2006
Haus der Kunst, Munich
8:30 pm

18 happenings in six parts by Allan Kaprow

Haus der Kunst
Prinzregentenstrasse 1
München
09/10/11 nov 2006
8:30 pm

Cast of participants

Serkan Salihoglu
who speaks and plays
a musical instrument
Judith Hummel
who speaks and moves
Mathilda Legemah
who moves and plays
a musical instrument
Jaume Villalba
who speaks, plays a game and
a musical instrument
Noémie Solomon
who moves and plays
a musical instrument
Maximilian Specketer
who moves, speaks and
plays a game
Two guest painters
each of whom paints
Florian Lauw and Valerie Masyuta
who set up objects
The visitors
who sit in various chairs

Instructions

The performance is divided into six parts. Each part contains three happenings which occur at once. The beginning and end of each will be signalled by a bell. At the end of the performance two strokes of the bell will be heard.

You have been given three cards. Be seated as they instruct you. That is, be sure to change your place for set three and set five.

Between part one and part two there is a *two minute* interval. Remain seated.

Between part two and part three there is a *fifteen minute* interval. You may move about freely.

Between part three and part four there is a *two minute* interval when you will remain in your seats.

Between part four and part five there is a *fifteen minute* interval. You may move about.

Between part five and part six there is a *two minute* interval. Remain seated.

There will be *no applause after each set.* You may applaud after the sixth set if you wish, although there will be no «curtain call».

The visitors are please asked not to smoke at all in the loft. They are also asked not to leave the building during the longer intermissions.

Handlungsanweisungen

Die Performance besteht aus 6 Teilen. Jeder Teil wiederum aus drei Happenings, die ohne Unterbrechung stattfinden. Der Anfang und das Ende jedes Happenings werden durch einen Glockenschlag markiert. Am Ende der Performance sind zwei Schläge der Glocke zu hören.

Sie haben drei Karten erhalten. Nehmen Sie so Platz, wie die Karten Sie anweisen. Wichtig ist, dass Sie Ihren Platz in den Pausen vor Teil drei und Teil fünf wechseln.

Zwischen Teil eins und Teil zwei gibt es *zwei Minuten* Pause. Bleiben Sie sitzen.

Zwischen Teil zwei und Teil drei gibt es eine *fünfzehnminütige* Pause. Sie dürfen sich frei bewegen.

Zwischen Teil drei und Teil vier gibt es *zwei Minuten* Pause, währenddessen Sie auf Ihren Plätzen bleiben.

Zwischen Teil vier und Teil fünf gibt es eine *fünfzehnminütige* Pause. Sie dürfen umher gehen.

Zwischen Teil *fünf* und Teil *sechs* gibt es *zwei Minuten* Pause. Bleiben Sie sitzen.

Es soll *zwischen den einzelnen Teilen nicht applaudiert werden.* Falls Sie es wünschen, dürfen Sie nach dem sechsten Teil applaudieren, auch wenn es keinen «Vorhang» gibt.

Die Besucher werden gebeten, nicht zu rauchen. Bitte verlassen Sie den Raum während der längeren Pausen nicht.

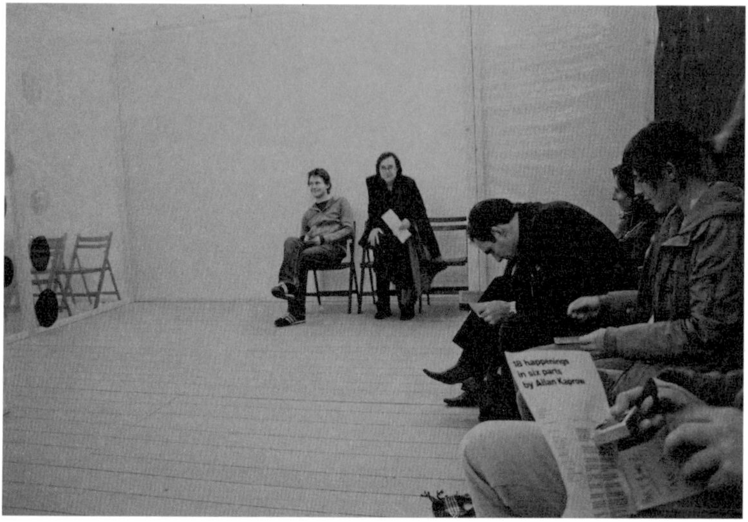

Room 3 / 08:30:00 pm

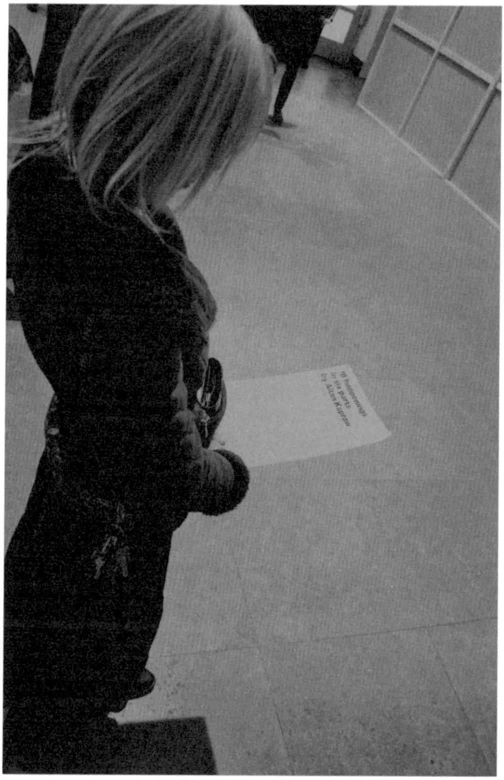

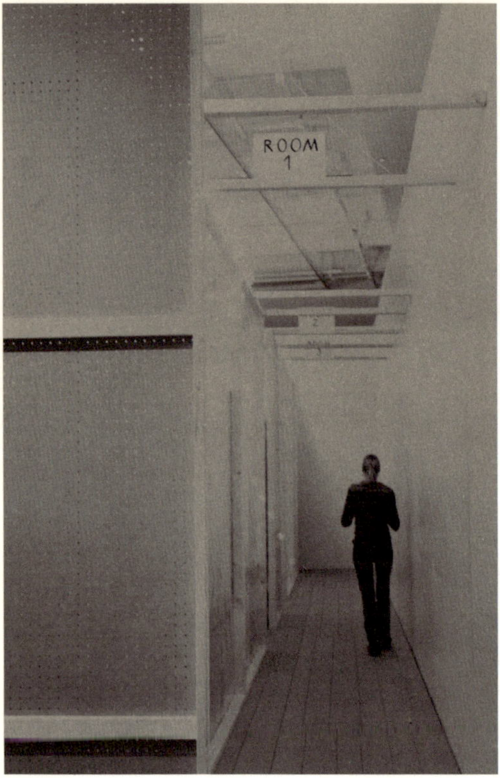

Corridor

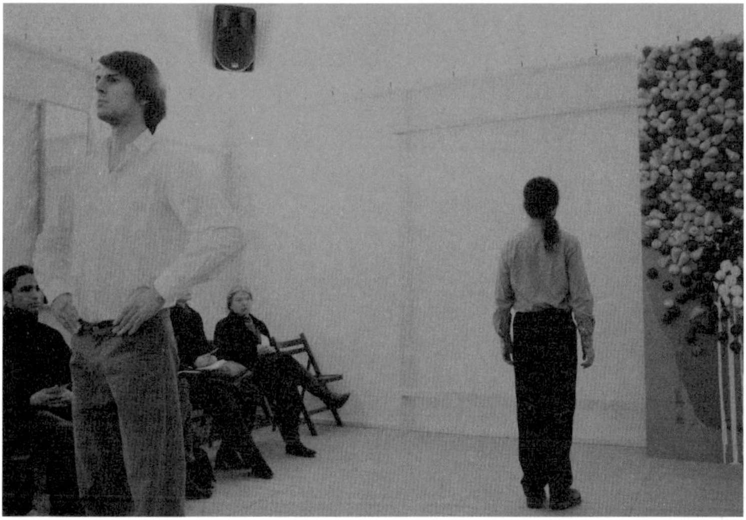

Room 1 / Set 1

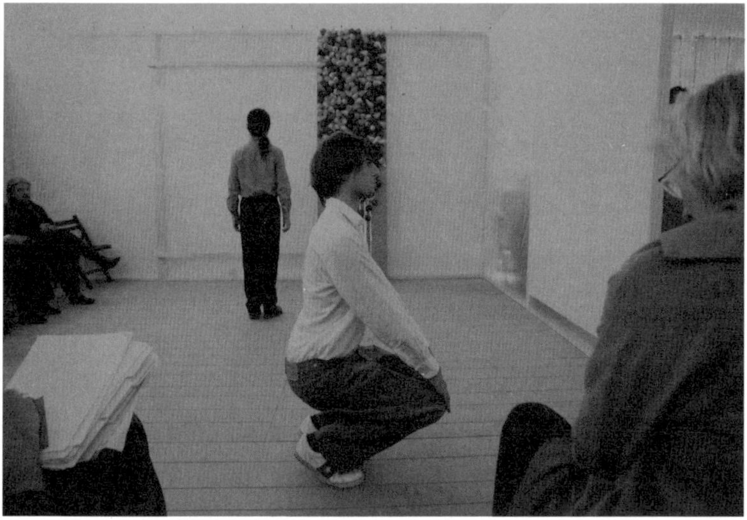

Room 1 / Set 1

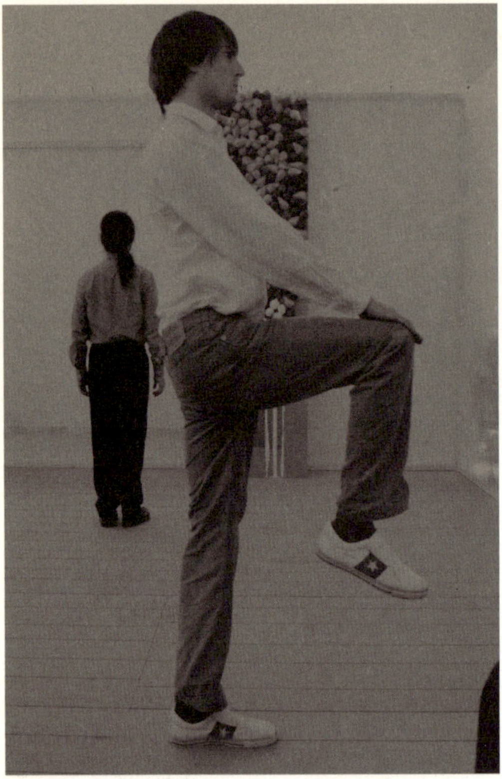

Room 1 / Set 1

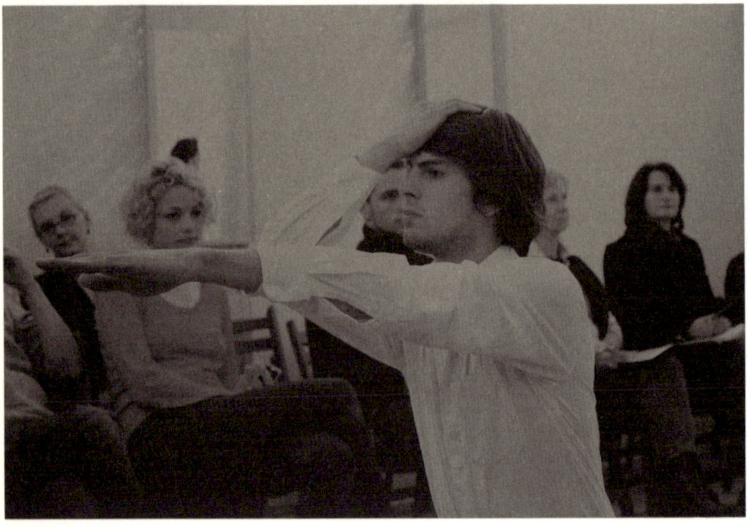

Room 1 / Set 1

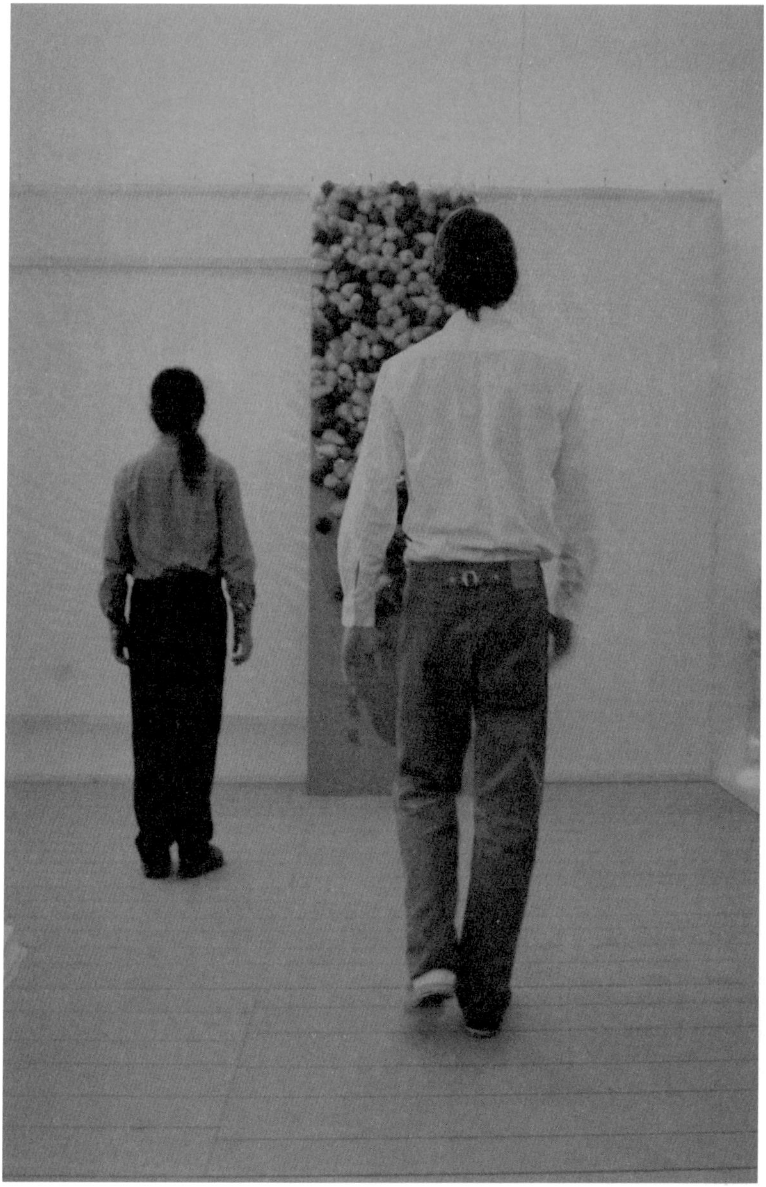

Room 1 / Set 1

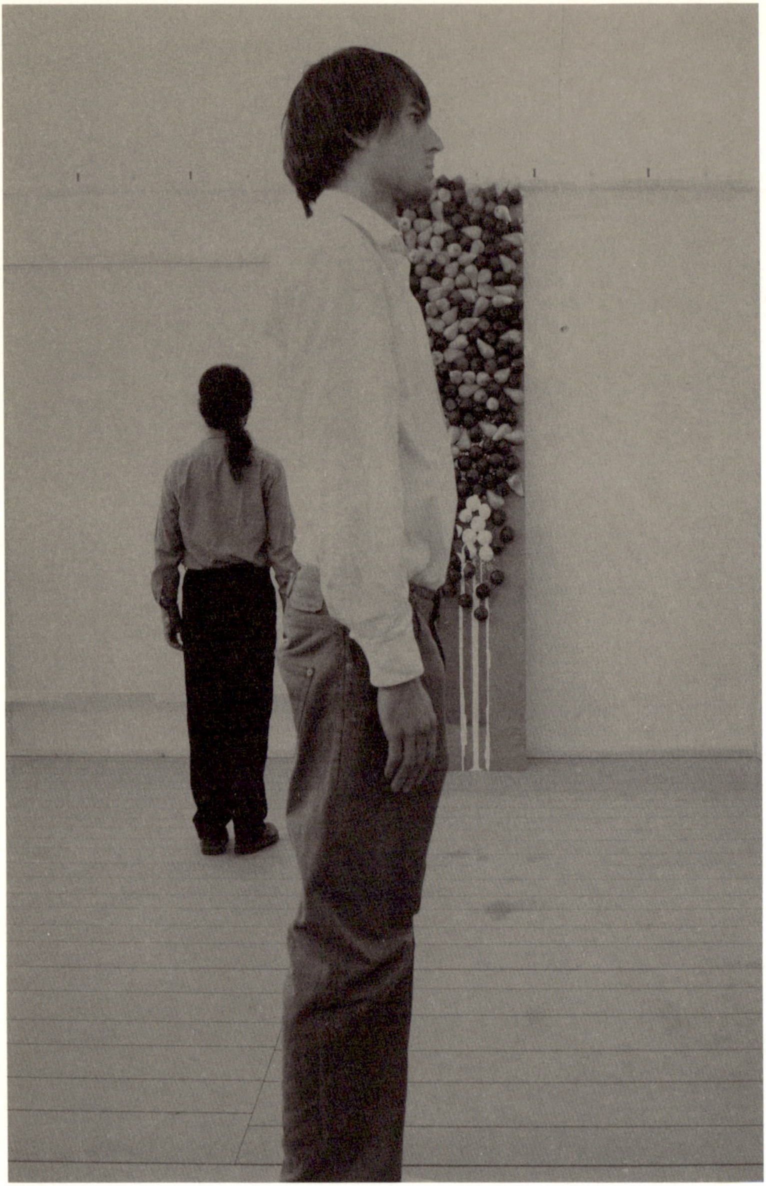

Room 1 / Set 1

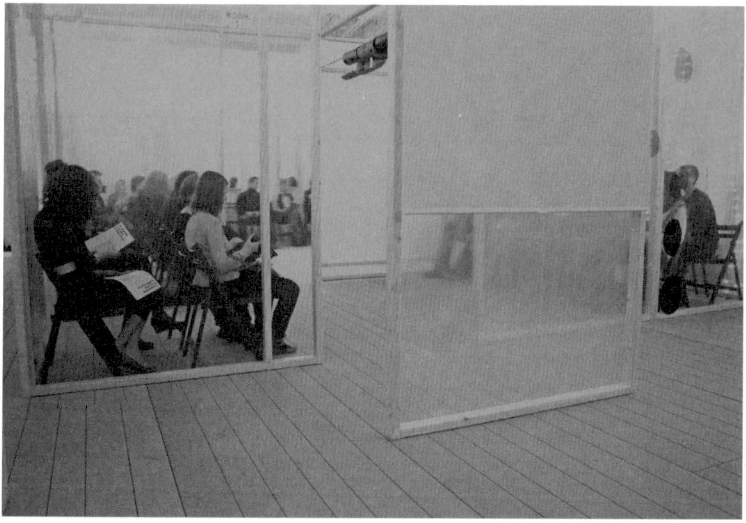

Rooms 3, 2 and 1 (seen from Room 3) / Pause #1

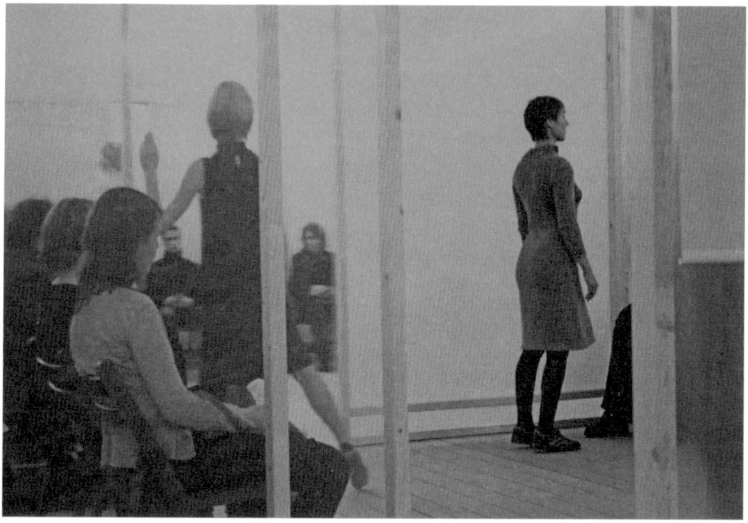

Room 2 / Set 1

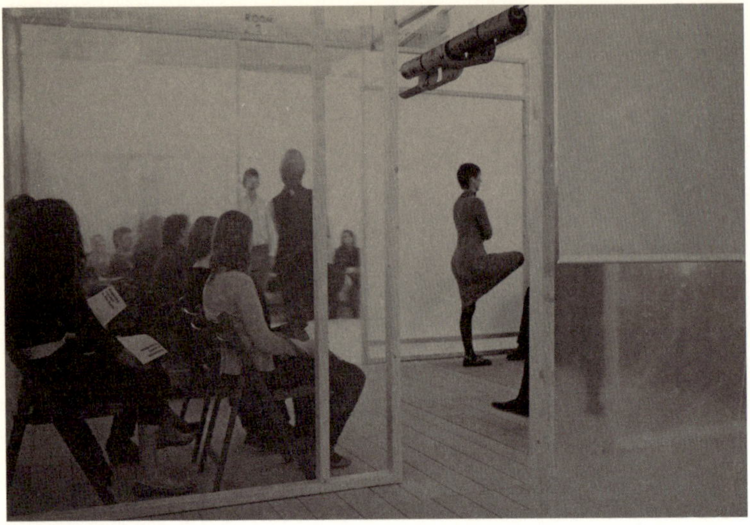

Room 2 / Set 1

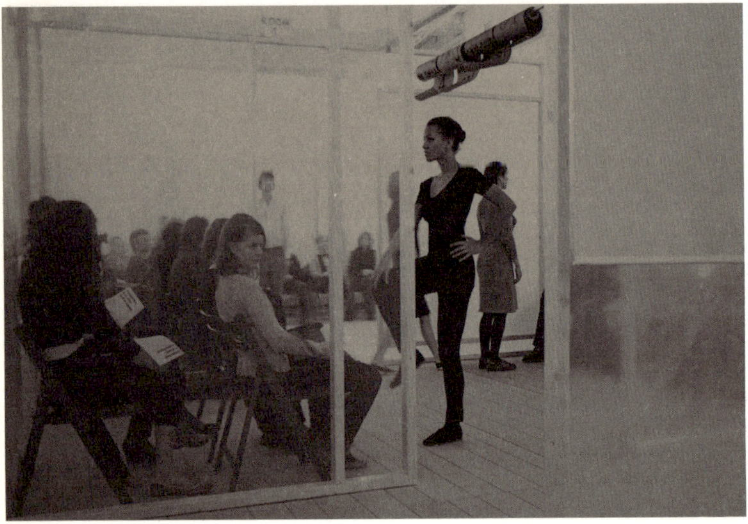

Room 2 / Set 1

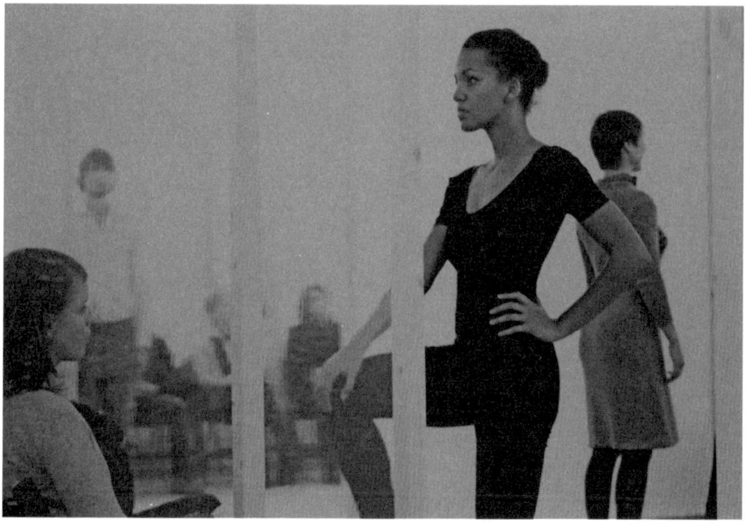

Room 2 / Set 1

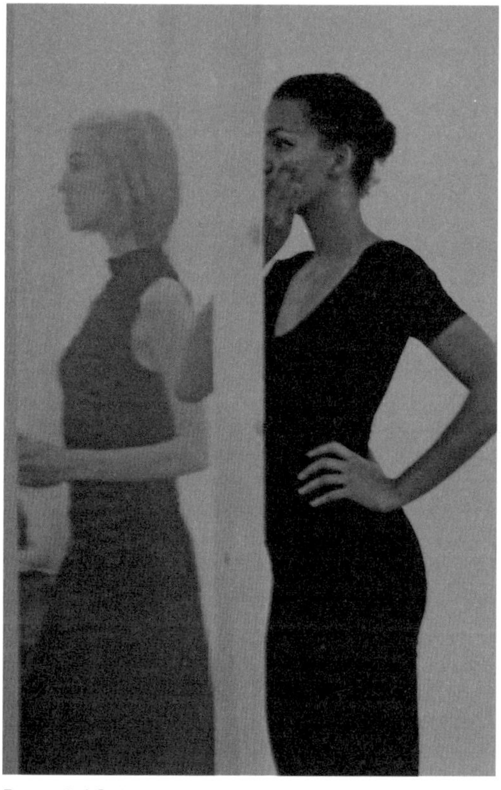

Room 2 / Set 1

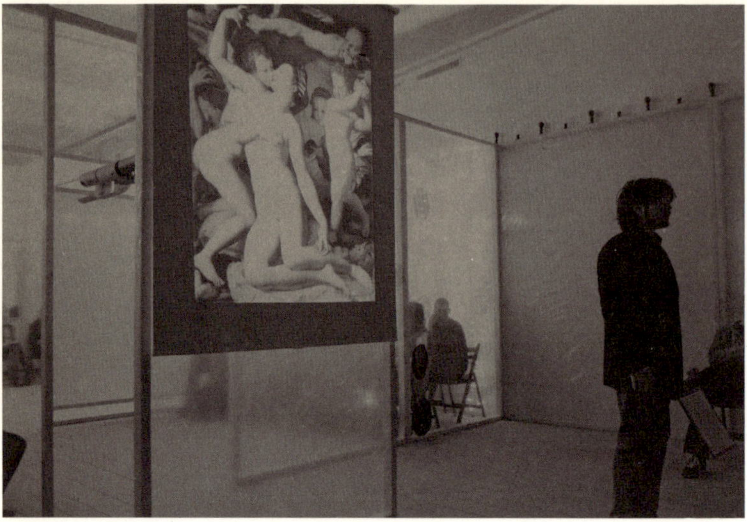
Room 3 / Set 2

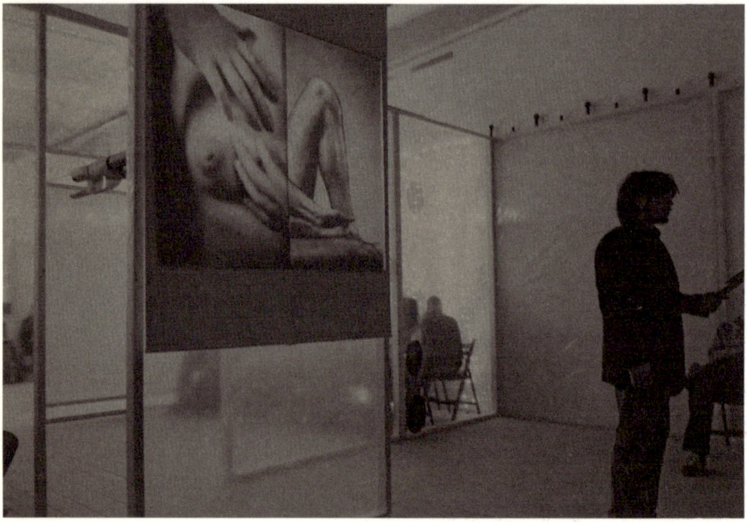
Room 3 / Set 2

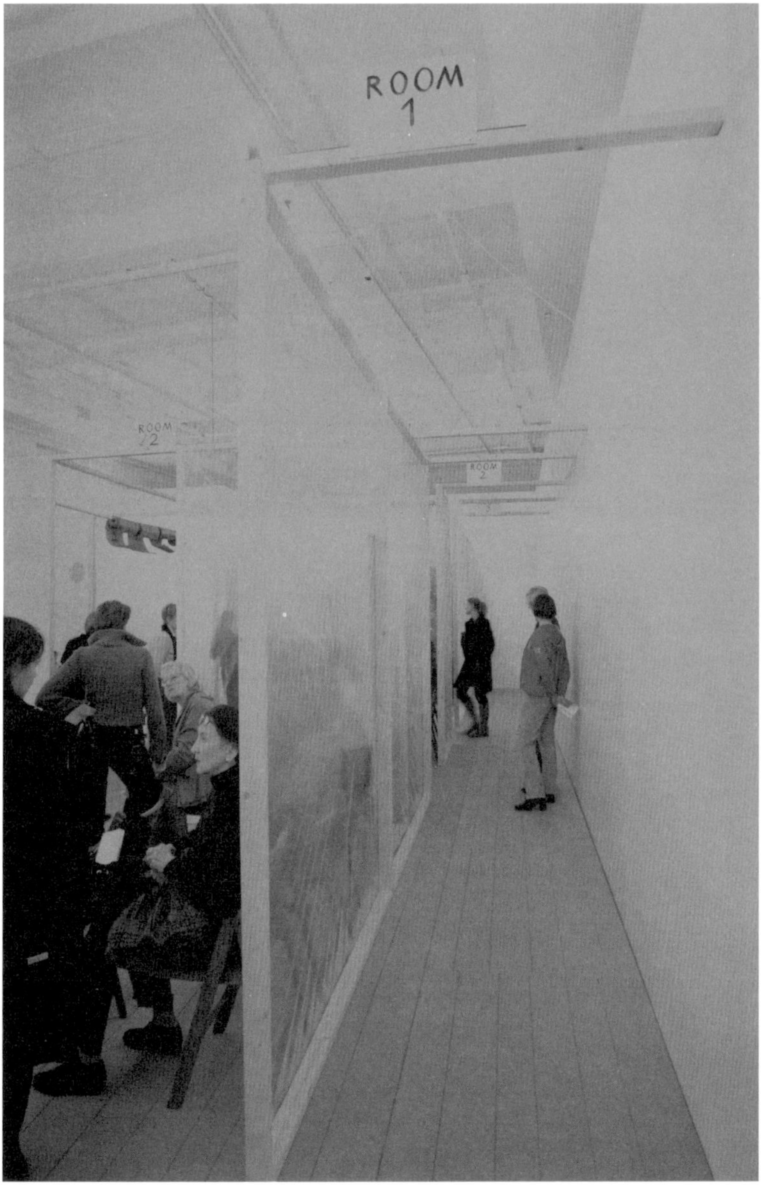

Corridor / Interval #1

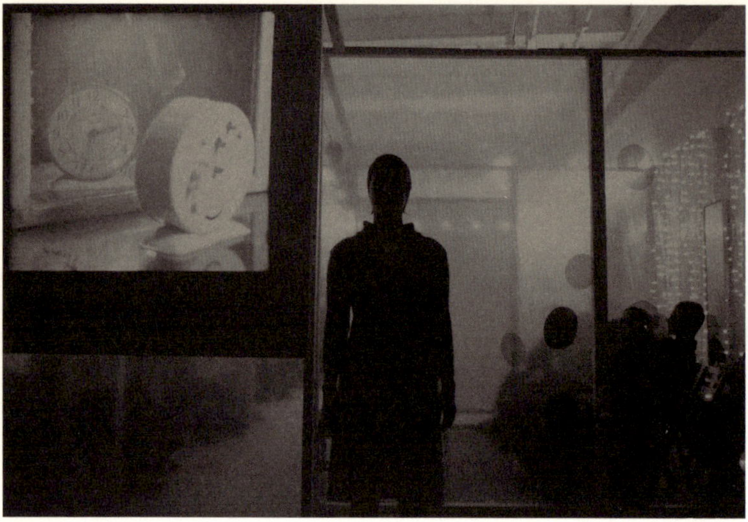

Room 3 / Set 3

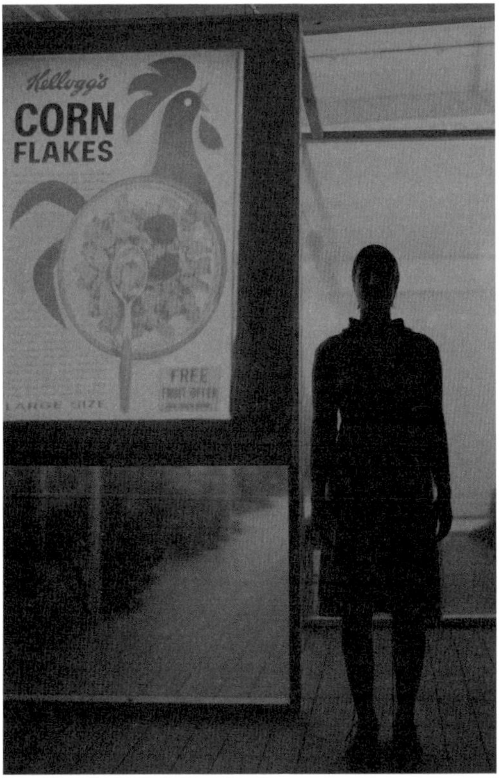

Room 3 / Set 3

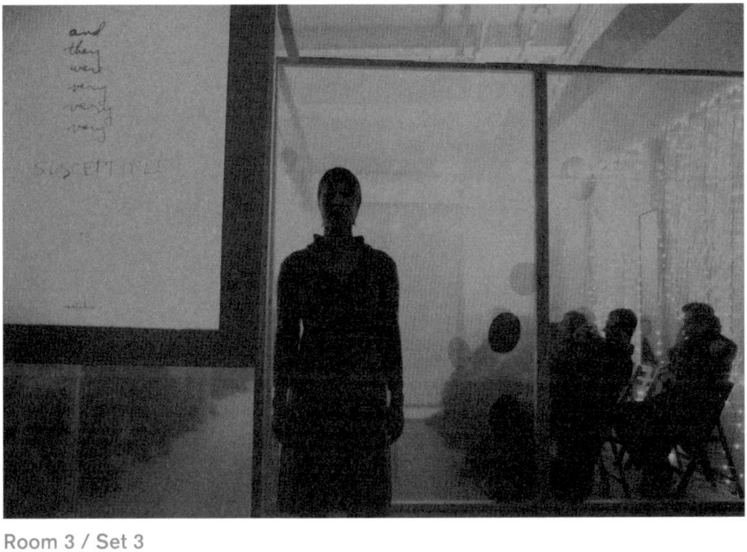

Room 3 / Set 3

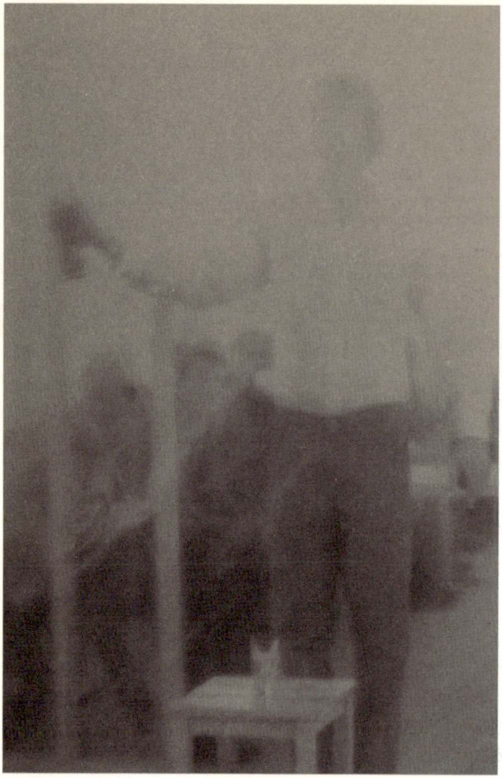

Room 3 / Set 4

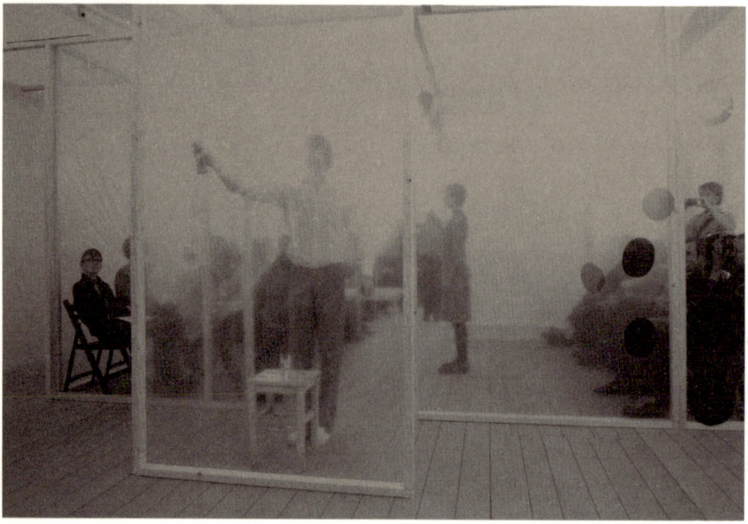

Room 3 / Set 4

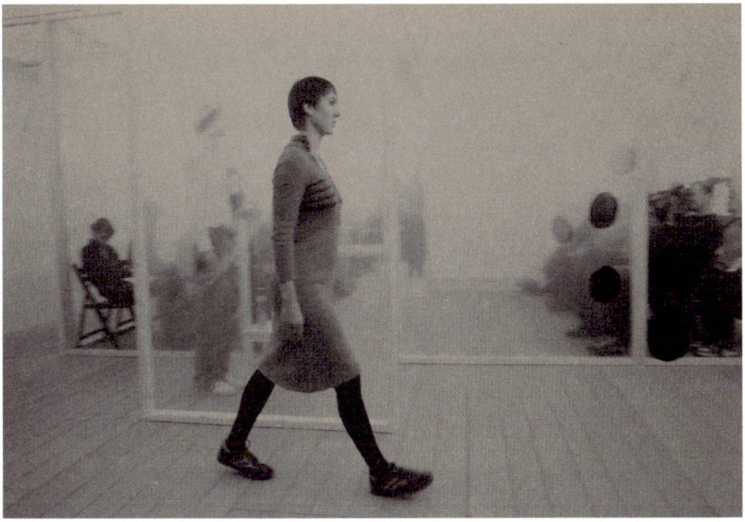

Room 3 / Set 4

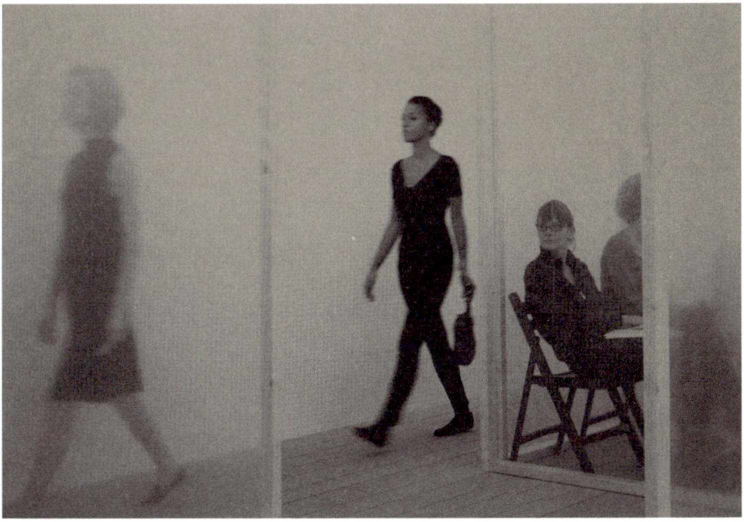

Corridor / Interval #2

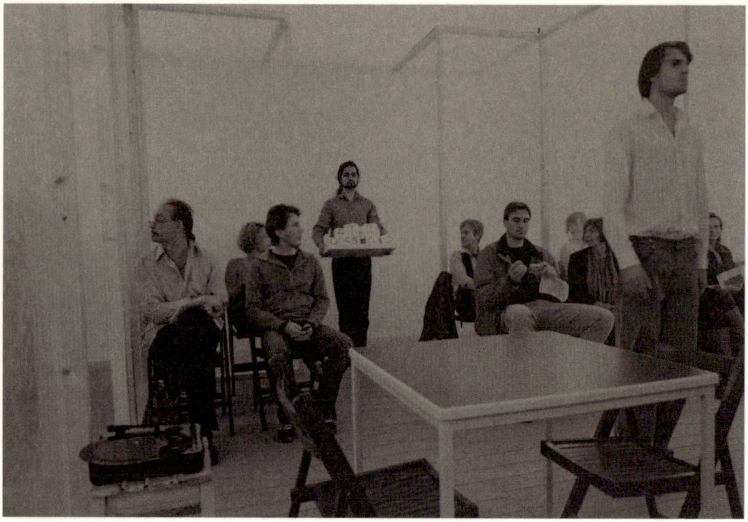

Room 2 / Set 3

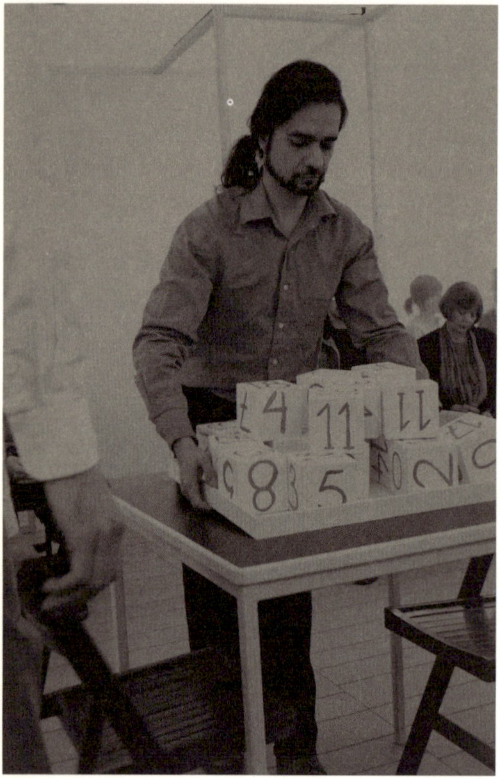

Room 2 / Set 3

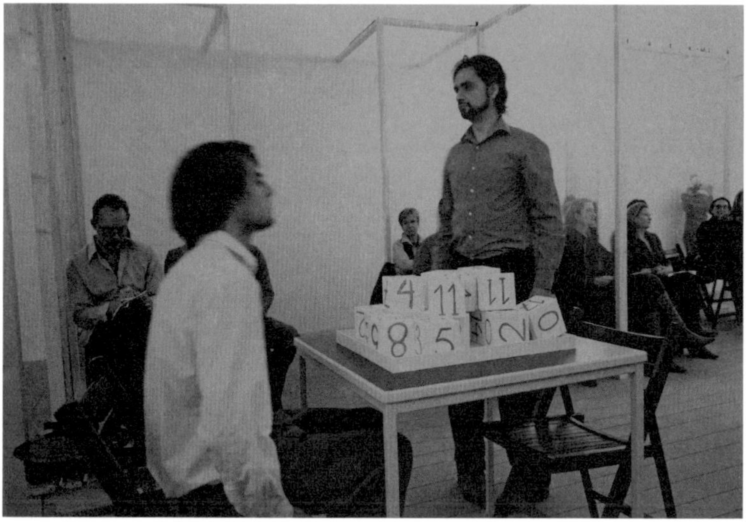

Room 2 / Set 3

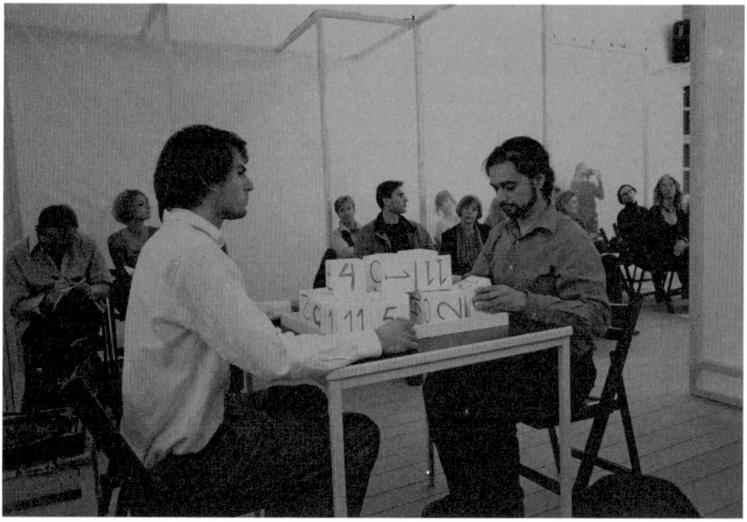

Room 2 / Set 3

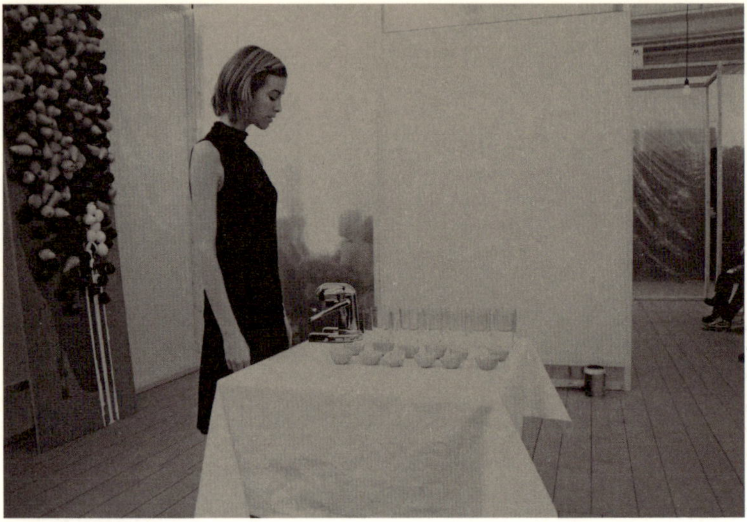
Room 1 / Set 5

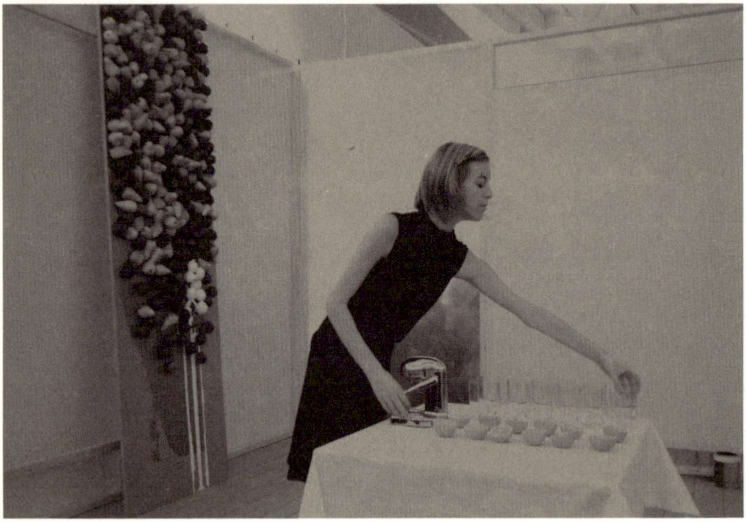
Room 1 / Set 5

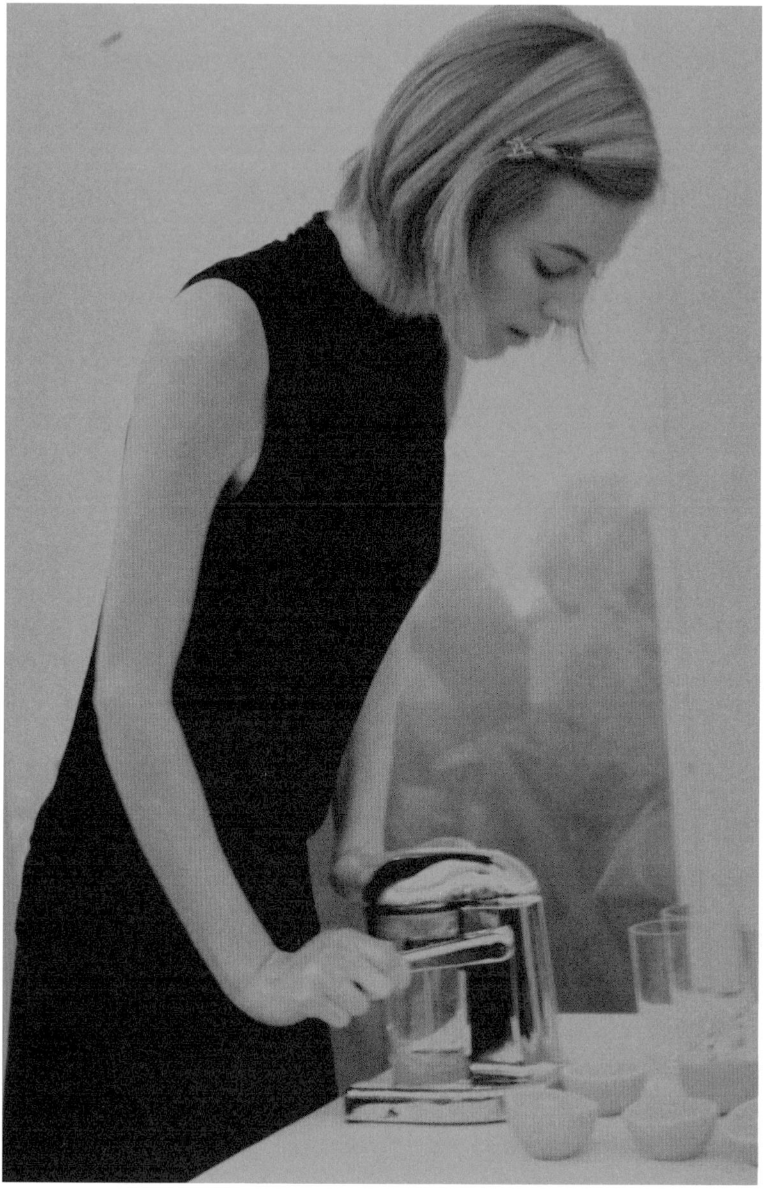

Room 1 / Set 5

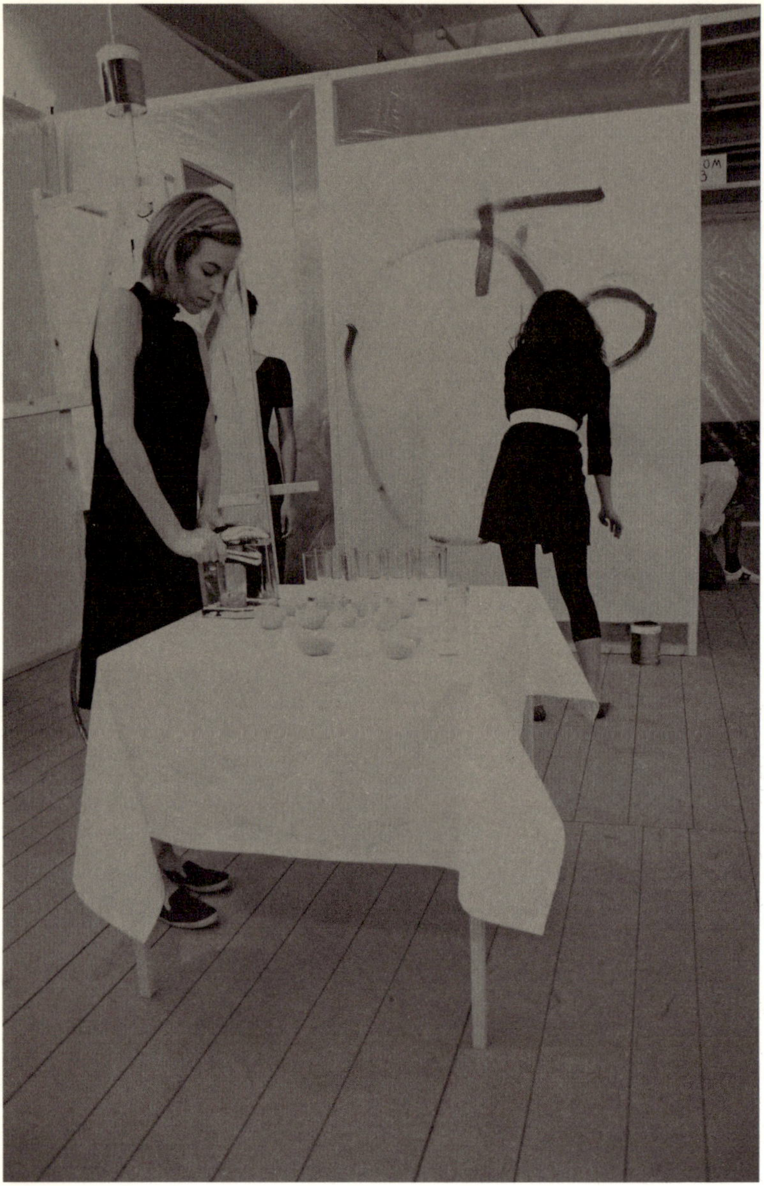

Room 1 / Set 5

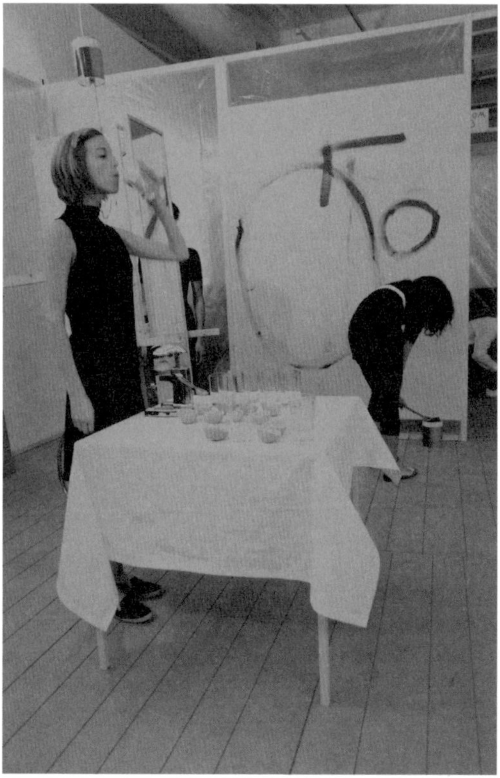

Room 1 / Set 5

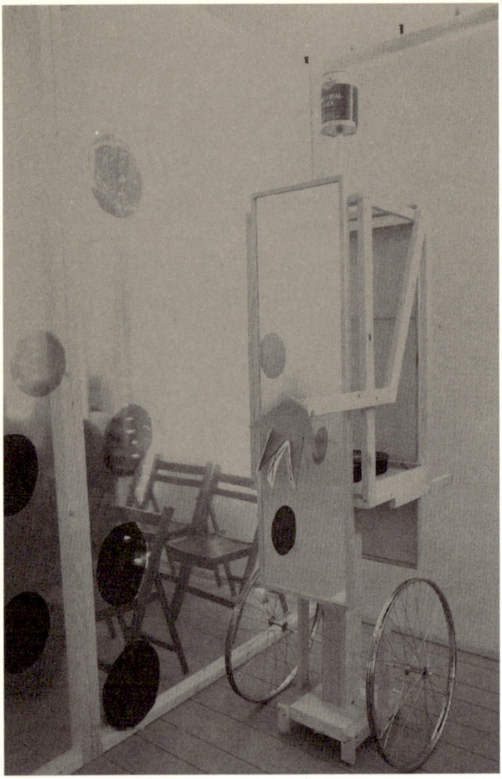

Room 3 / Interval #2

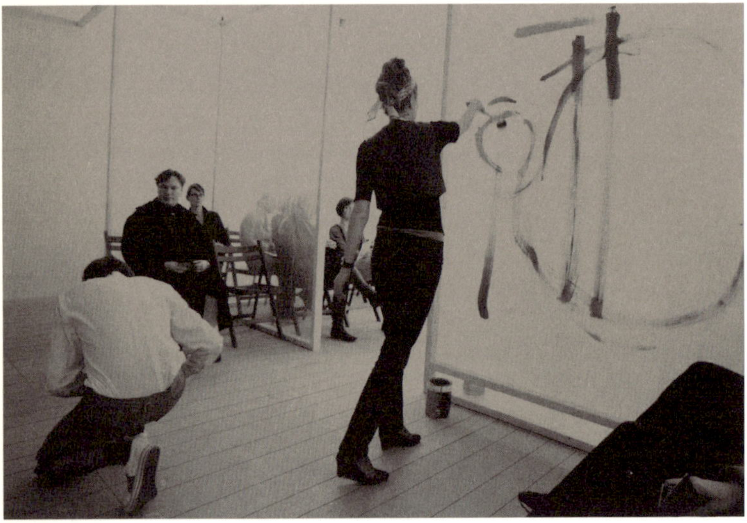

Room 2 / Set 5

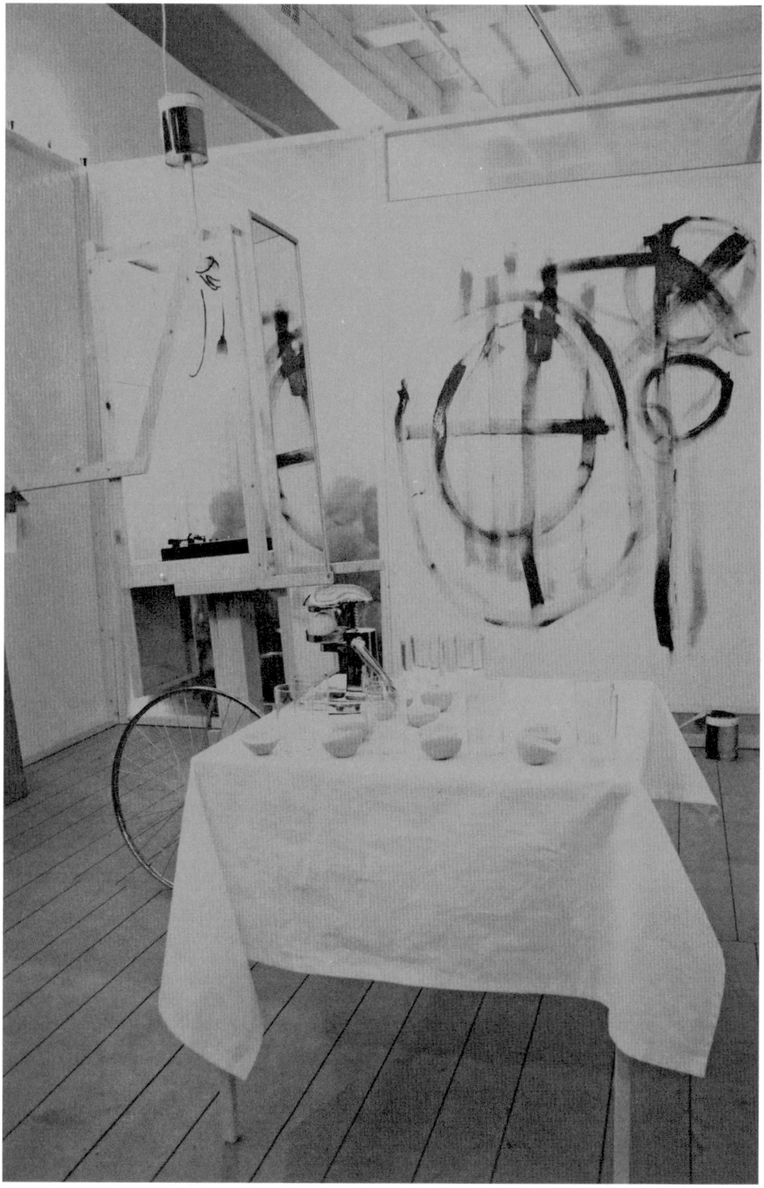

Room 1 / Set 6

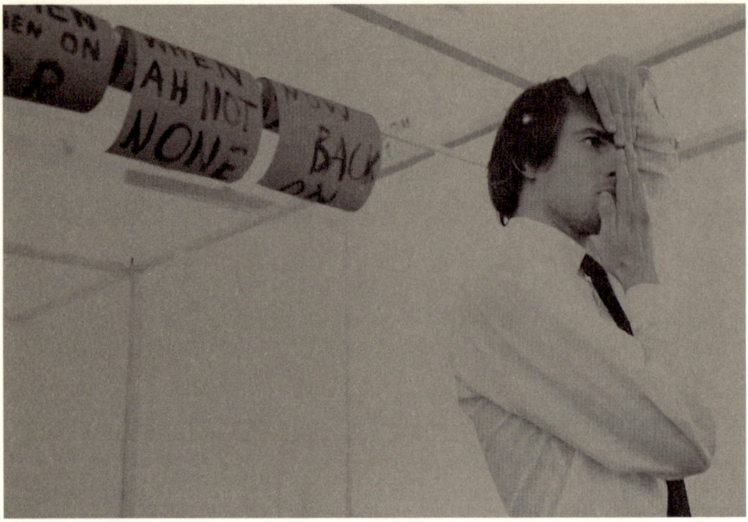

Room 2 / Set 5

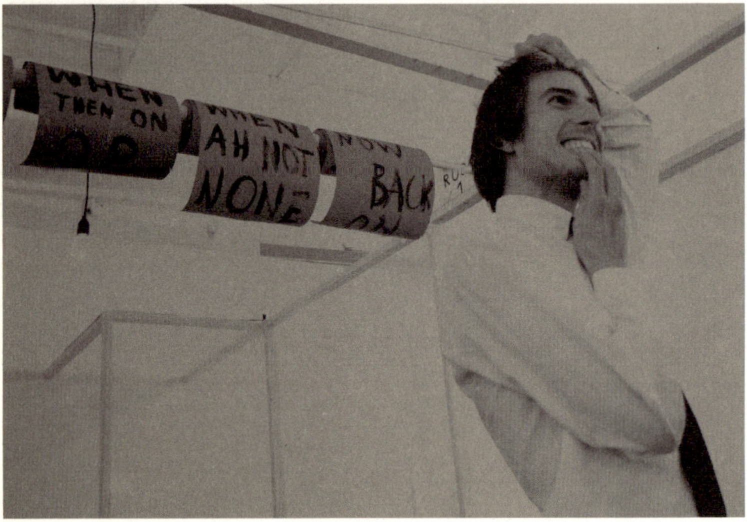

Room 2 / Set 5

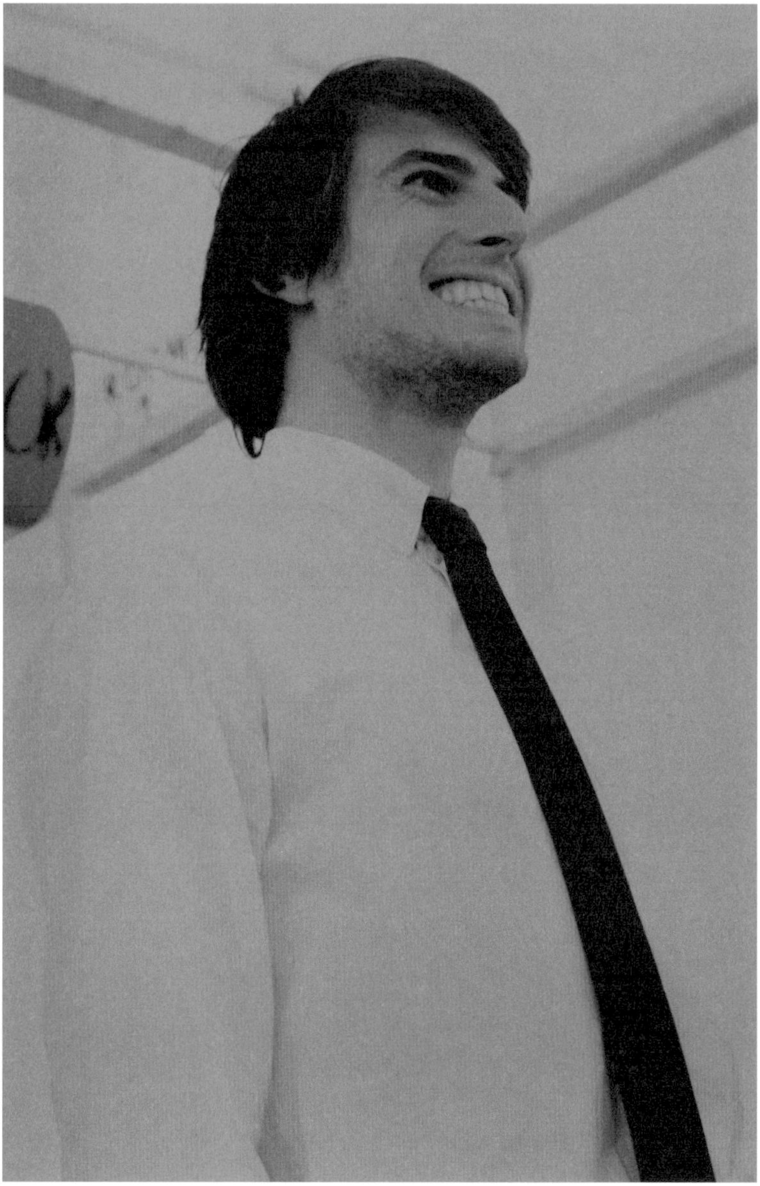

Room 2 / Set 5

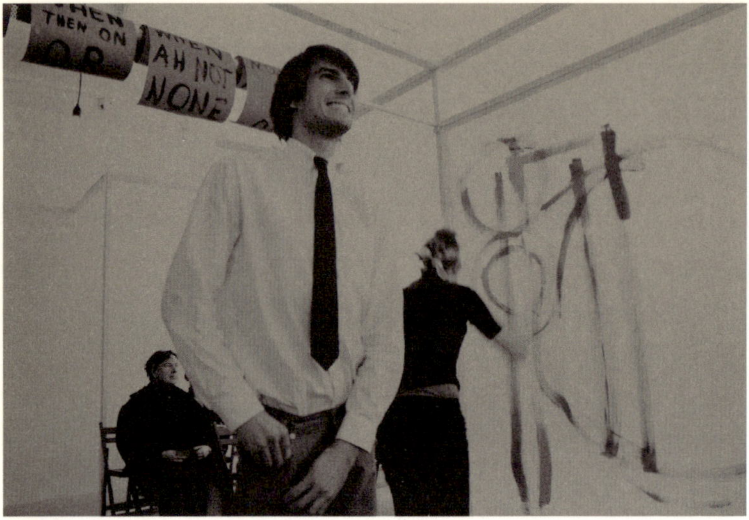

Room 2 / Set 5

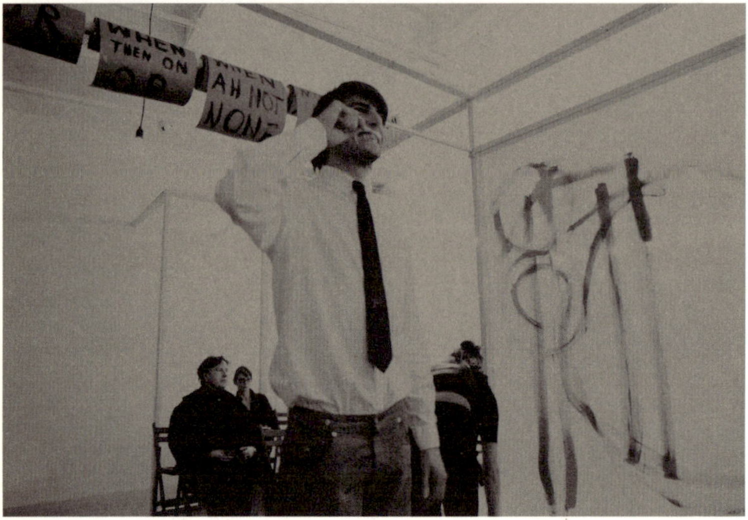

Room 2 / Set 5

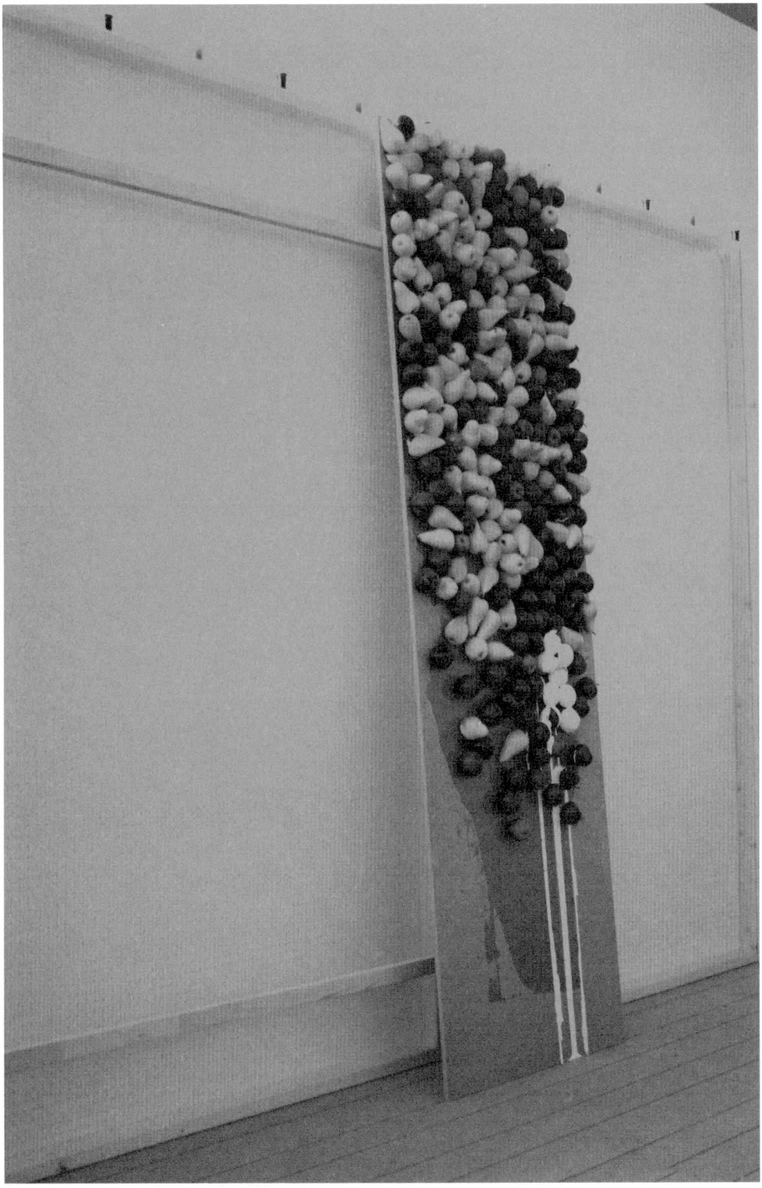

Room 1

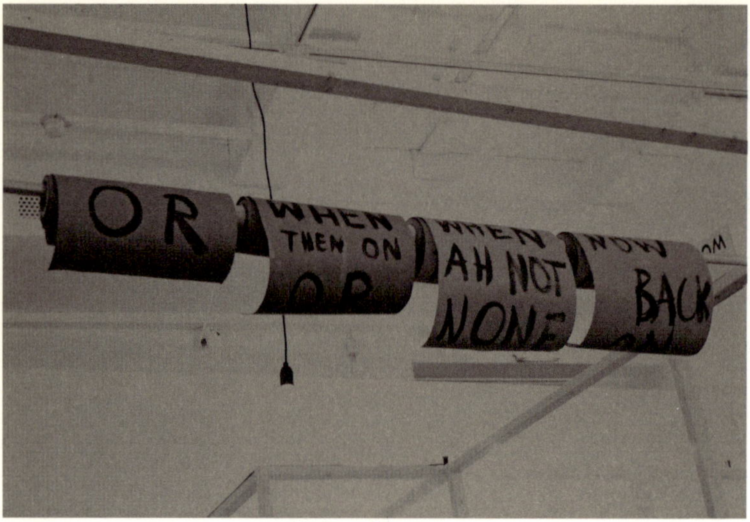

Room 2

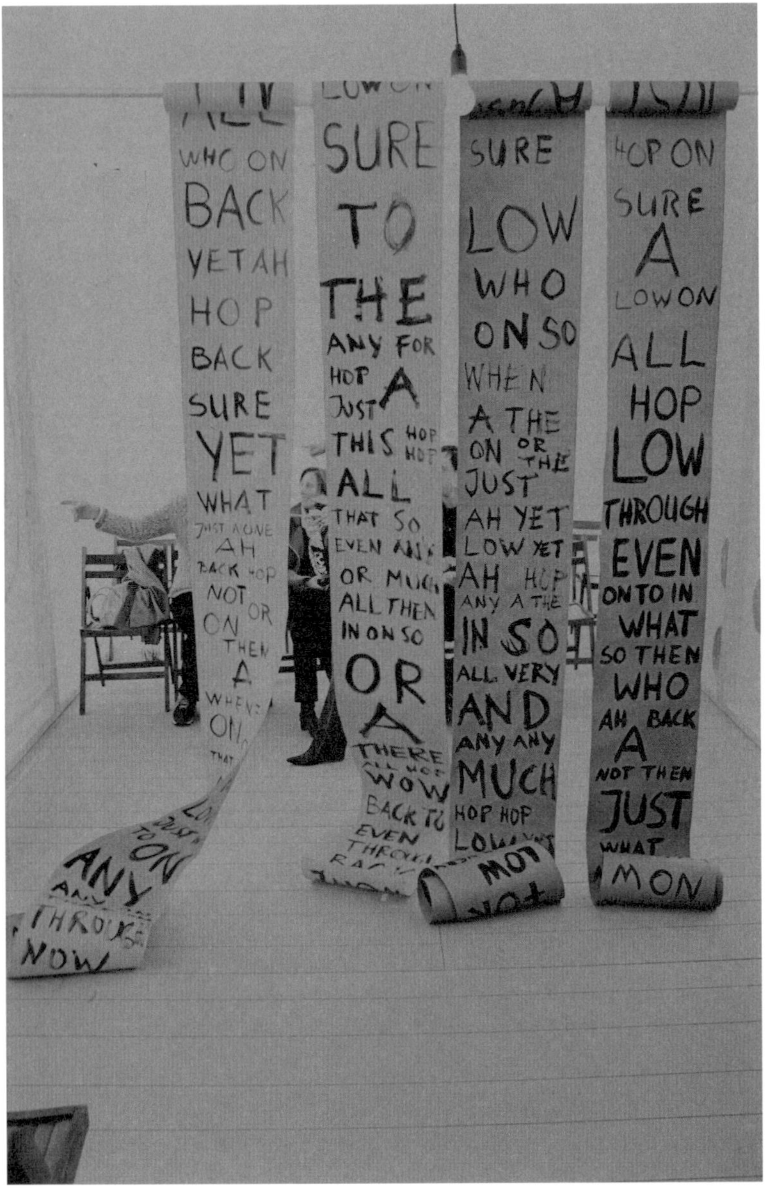

Finis / 09:30:15 pm

REDOING 18 HAPPENINGS IN 6 PARTS

André Lepecki

1

——— At the end of a densely scribbled page-and-a-half summary of *18 Happenings in 6 Parts*—a summary probably written right before public performances were about to start on 4 October 1959, and which includes last-minute cast modifications, new timings for some of the acts, brief sound descriptions, and clarifications of actions—Kaprow wrote:

"Each of these parts may be re-arranged indefinitely."

Thus, at least in October of 1959, as he was about to make history, Kaprow registered his desire for future actualizations of *18 Happenings in 6 Parts*—indefinitely opened ones, for sure; but still composed by meticulously arranged "parts."

2

——— When Stephanie Rosenthal invited me to co-curate and direct a redoing of *18 Happenings in 6 Parts* for the Kaprow exhibition at Haus der Kunst, Munich, I hesitated. At the time, I had not yet seen Kaprow's detailed choreographic scores, nor had I examined the approximately four hundred sheets of notes, drawings, texts, poems, sketches, manifestos, fundraising letters, and cryptic technical exchanges with sound engineers. I had not seen Kaprow's very peculiar fingering instructions for flute and violin (Part Four, Room One), nor had I read his outrageously funny ideas for costumes (he never used them in performance) or his descriptions of some of the slides to be projected in room three during each "act" or "part" or "set" (Kaprow used these interchangeably throughout his notes). I had not known then that the twenty-four minutes and fifteen seconds of rigorously timed events comprising the six parts were also rigorously framed by a total of thirty-six minutes of timed "non-events"—intervals and pauses occupying more time in the performance than the carefully planned actions themselves. Nor did I know of Kaprow's desire to have *Helena Polka* blasting away at a certain point in Part Five, Room One—at the precise moment when two guest painters simultaneously action-paint vertical and horizontal lines on the two sides of an unprimed canvas dividing Room One from Room Two. I had not read his amazingly beautiful text on time, delivered by Kaprow himself in Room One, Part Two. And, of course, I had not yet read his plan to dispatch *18 Happenings in 6 Parts* to unknown futures...

3

——— All I knew of *18 Happenings in 6 Parts* was pretty much what is generally known about it: that it was a groundbreaking work responsible for bringing that felicitous word "Happening" into the vocabulary of twentieth-century performance; that apparently John Cage had disliked it quite a bit (and that Kaprow had been quite disappointed by Cage's reaction); that Michael Kirby had published a very meticulous description of it (which immediately became, and remains today, *the* discursive proxy for the event); that *18 Happenings in 6 Parts* had inaugurated the Reuben Gallery in New York, a venue where some budding names of post-modern dance would soon come to perform; that Robert Rauschenberg and Jasper Johns had participated in it; that Samuel Delaney had stumbled upon it while walking on Fourth Avenue on an October evening and had most probably been the only black teenager among the very exclusive Manhattan art crowd. But most of all, I vividly recalled an influential critical essay by Kaprow, "Happenings in the New York Scene," published in 1961, two years after he had created *18 Happenings in 6 Parts*, and where he clearly defined Happenings as "events that, put simply, happen…they exist for a single performance, or only a few, and are gone forever as new ones take their place." [1]

Because of that clear-cut definition, my first impulse was to refuse the invitation. Indeed, how could anyone return to a piece that was so iconic, but that had also been so radically set aside by its own author? Kaprow had even made the point to create, in 1988, a series of Happenings under the same title that purposefully had nothing in common with the original—a return to the 1959 version, he stated, would be both "dull" and "totally uninteresting to engage again today." [2] In light of all this, my question was: how to redo a piece when the *perception* we have of it today is of an extraordinarily innovative idea that somehow did not turn out as well as it should in its first incarnation—as opposed to other Happenings Kaprow would create later, such as *A Spring Happening* (1961), *Self-Service* (1966), or *Fluids* (1967). Indeed, art critics at the time either ignored it (Kaprow's papers at the Getty include an unfinished letter to Hilton Kramer asking the art critic to explain his absence from *18 Happenings in 6 Parts*); or thought of it as a badly put together entertainment. Fairfield Porter concluded his two-column review for *The Nation* with these devastating sentences: "Avant-garde art has the merit of surprise. Kaprow's avant-garde 'event' constantly disappoints one's expectation of surprise. Like so many science fiction movies about the future, his subject matter is the undigested immediate past."

So, why eventually agree to direct a redoing of *18 Happenings in 6 Parts*? First and foremost: Kaprow's extraordinarily generous personal consent. This was the crucial event in my decision-making process. And then, after going over Kaprow's notes, the realization that what is widely described in the scholarship as "the script" or "the

---

1 Allan Kaprow and Jeff Kelley, Essays on the Blurring of Art and Life, Berkeley 2003.
2 Quotes taken from a sound file, courteously provided by Peter Kirby, of a preparatory meeting for the 1988 version of 18 Happenings in 6 Parts in New York. In that file we can hear Kaprow briefly discussing the 1959 version.

score" for *18 Happenings in 6 Parts* is rather a massive textual and visual work, almost autonomous in itself in its prolific poetic ramifications and performative potentialities. One could even say that a significant part of the materialization of those eighteen Happenings takes place only on paper; they belong exclusively to paper, words and drawings and sketches performing away on dozens upon dozens of pages. On paper, *18 Happenings in 6 Parts* is a dynamic, truly rhizomatic collection of virtual ideas, beautiful poems, impossible actions, architectural dreams, sharp, short manifestos on art, music, and theater, hilariously self-aggrandizing narratives, hilariously self-deprecating narratives, brilliantly compact theoretical texts, insightful quasi-ethnographic snapshots of quotidian expressions, acute diagnostics on urban life, heartbreaking confessions of the artist before the huge challenges posed by the project.

4

———Amid this virtual performance that takes place on paper rather than in space, we can find a couple of dozen pages which are clearly aimed at preserving and transmitting a rigorous performance structure and a rigorous choreographic score (including the page-and-a-half summary cited at the beginning of this text). Yet, even these rigorous notes were always, and constitutively, slightly "anexact;" i.e. not really inexact, but beside or beyond the problem of exactitude. Indeed, Kaprow's movement and sound scores, despite their meticulousness, were fraught with small inaccuracies and micro-paradoxes. In their rigorous delivery Kaprow had certainly (purposefully?) left some room to play—a playfulness allowed by the indeterminacy of language, as in the detailed "technical instructions" Kaprow handed to the two technicians running sound and slides in the hidden "control room," right behind the large assemblage in Room Three. With the heading "TECHNICIANS: INSTRUCTIONS" and the footer "FINIS," these guide the cadence of slides throughout the performance thus:

———Act 1: 16 Slides (rapidly)
———Act 3: 13 Slides (rapidly)
———Act 4: 11 Slides (fast)
———Act 5: 9 Slides (quickly)

Soon I realized that to redo *18 Happenings in 6 Parts* would be to constantly delve into problems similar to the one of finding out exactly what could be the difference between doing something "rapidly" and doing something "quickly"—and then finding out the additional difference between these two and doing something "fast." Thus, I kept as my main dramaturgical guideline the following formula: all instructions and scores, all choreographic details so carefully annotated by Kaprow, were to be approached (precisely) as being "rigorous yet anexact" instructions. That this apparently paradoxical formula is also the one used by Gilles Deleuze to describe the dynamics of organic life, I took as being more than mere coincidence.

5

——— The first issue to solve was that of space; rather, that of *place*—of where to place the redoing. Stephanie and I immediately agreed that we had to rebuild with as much accuracy as possible the precarious architecture Kaprow had created within the Reuben Gallery: three rooms separated by walls of semi-transparent plastic film, connected by openings between the rooms, and by a corridor running along the whole length of the structure. This had some difficulties, the major one being the lack of a ground plan. But very quickly Christin Vahl (the architect who, early on, became part of our creative team, also responsible for creating all the artwork installed in the redoing) and I deduced the dimensions of the rooms from photographs of the 1959 performance. The layering of semi-transparent walls, the opacity and scale of the assemblages in Rooms One and Three, the reflective surfaces of the five full-body mirrors in two of the rooms, the combination of clear, almost modernist lines with the precariousness and cheap quality of the materials, the vaudeville-like red, white, and blue light bulbs: all proposed an environment that I felt had to be directly related, symbiotically related, to Kaprow's angular, minimalist choreography. Architecture was movement and movement was architecture: precise and precarious, orthogonal and simple.

But the true problem in terms of space was neither that of figuring out correct dimensions nor of overcoming the lack of an original ground plan. The real problem was that we would be placing *18 Happenings in 6 Parts* inside a museum's gallery—when it was clear that its original location inside an empty loft on Fourth Avenue in Manhattan's East Village was already Kaprow's critique of how art gets to be framed, consumed, accessed.

So, the problem was how to de-territorialize our room from the institutional frame of the museum. Once I learned that the large Terrassensaal gallery had been assigned for the redoing at Haus der Kunst, I wrote this to Christin: "But I have this vision of building a big wooden box, 8m x 14m x 3m, where someone outside would only see a bunch of cables coming in and out from several places. One small step, a door, and inside the whole atmosphere of 18/6." The aim was to create an object in space that would reveal neither itself nor its contents fully—nor give itself to be viewed or contemplated at a distance as a work of art. Moreover, I wanted to place this huge box at an angle, so that it wouldn't align with the structure of the building: the redoing could only take place inside a museum's gallery as long as it remained slightly misplaced. Christin responded brilliantly to this idea by conceiving a large structure made out of cheap construction materials with porous outside walls, like a skin. Plain wood on the outside, painted white on the inside, roofless. I found her solution perfect.

Sitting by the wall near the entrance in Room One, looking up, the misalignment of our box with the rest of the building generated a slight sensation of vertigo.

A second problem was that of casting. It was clear we wanted to work with art students.[3] The performers would have to be aware of the fact they would need to unlearn their training (if any) and accept Kaprow's intelligent simplicity. I asked Noémie Solomon, choreographer and dance scholar, working on her doctorate on dance and notation at New York University, to take on the crucial task of decoding Kaprow's scores and actualizing them into movement, identifying overall rhythms, movement patterns, and then teaching them. She also performed in the redoing, and was assistant to the director.

One detail required a major decision to be made in terms of casting. In Kirby's description of the performers, we learn they were "dressed in ordinary street clothes (a Negro girl wore a black leotard)..." This anachronistic mode of reference to one of the performers took me directly to the very specific period of the late 1950s in US history. Given the way Kaprow controlled with absolute precision every single detail of the production, the differentiation between the "Negro girl" in her skin-tight leotard and the other performers, in street clothes, was certainly purposeful—in contrast with the others, we could see her physical presence as being more like a "human figure,"[4] pictorially reified throughout art history as male and white. This could not be taken as a small detail in the work of a sculptor and a painter so invested in critiquing the history of Western art (a critique that *18 Happenings in 6 Parts* partakes fully). It was quite a statement in 1959 at the height of the civil rights movement, and given the lack of *visibility* of black women in avant-garde circles in New York (and, in part, in the visual arts, of black men—see Delaney's account in his memoirs). In casting the redoing I would have to take into consideration the ways Kaprow was approaching the politics of racial visibility and invisibility.[5] In the redoing, the "Negro girl" could not be replaced by just anybody.

Another performance element corroborated this decision: a mechanical toy. Kirby describes how a man "entered the second room [Part 4], put the mechanical toy on the table and set it in motion. About one foot high, it was the brightly colored figure of a Negro dancing on a drum; the legs jiggled and swung frantically when the toy

3 We were helped in this process by Professor Jörg von Brincken from the Ludwig-Maximilians-Universität in Munich. The performers were: Judith Hummel, Mathilda Legemah, Jaume Villalba Sanchez, Serkan Salihoglu, Noémie Solomon, Maximilian Specketer. Coryl Kaprow replaced Noémie in Parts Four and Five on two evenings. We were very fortunate to have worked with them.

4 In 1959 that "Negro girl" was Shirley Prendergast.

5 In the unpublished letter to Fairfield Porter mentioned above, Kaprow accuses the reviewer of being incapable of properly seeing what surrounds him. Kaprow phrases his accusation by making an analogy between the art critic and "... the British who goes to Hong Kong for the first time and sees his house-boy everywhere he goes, on every street corner, tens of thousands of examples of this poor wretch—concluding that the Chinese are all alike ..."

was started." Throughout his notes, Kaprow calls this toy "Black Sambo"—a crucial character in the history of that foundational form of US popular entertainment, blackface minstrelsy, and in the history of US racism. Again, the inclusion of this Sambo dancing mechanically to the cacophony of an avant-garde orchestra playing in the next room in an environment lit by red, white, and blue light bulbs was not an innocent gesture in 1959. For the redoing, a decision had to be made about what mechanical toy to use. For a while I considered buying an antique (there are plenty of tin toy Sambos available on eBay). But this would be as if the visual economy of racism and of blackness, as mechanized subjectivity always ready to provide pure entertainment, were a thing of the past. Walking on the streets of Rio de Janeiro, I stumbled upon the solution, literally on the evening before taking my plane to Munich. The colorful, twelve-inch-tall "Rap Brother" faced me from behind a window in a toy store in Ipanema—thick red lips, maniacal grin, gloved hands. Just press his wrist and he hip-hops endlessly, upon command. He flew to Munich with me and performed the redoing with us every night.

Last element to solve: sound. Kaprow's notes mention that the whole environment was crossed by a quadraphonic system, rendering a complex electronic composition. But without any detailed information other than Kaprow's loose description of his electronic music in different annotations as "high pitched," or "very compact," or a "jumble of words," it was very hard at first to imagine how to redo the sound score. We did have the unfinished three-page hand-written text addressed "TO THE THEATRE PEOPLE," (subtitled "Innovator") in which Kaprow described (in the third person) the sound work for *18 Happenings in 6 Parts* as "pure essences rather than 'music' in the conventional sense." In another fragment, Kaprow describes his music work as based on the principle of treating sounds not as notes but as self-contained "events," thus allowing him to create music that was void of any "compositional" concerns. I asked composer Shawn Greenlee, working at Brown University on his doctorate on the relation between electronic music and image, to be responsible for the sound design of the redoing. Then we got lucky. Peter Kirby contacted us. He had found a box containing the five tapes used by Kaprow in 1959. Our task of decoding Kaprow's intentions became easier—even though the discovery of the tapes also made clear that all sounds had to be constantly arranged and re-arranged in real time throughout the performance: the tapes were to be played like an instrument, which resulted in a more dynamic sound environment. In performance, Shawn played with Kaprow's "pure essences" every night.

6

——— Each of these parts may be re-arranged indefinitely.

———

André Lepecki is Associate Professor in Performance Studies at New York University.

ART AS LIFE

KUNST ALS LEBEN
Haus der Kunst, Munich, October 2006–January 2007
KUNST ALS LEVEN
Van Abbemuseum, Eindhoven, Feburary–April 2007

55 ——— Installation view
Haus der Kunst, Munich
56 ——— Installation view
Haus der Kunst, Munich
58 ——— Installation view
Van Abbemuseum, Eindhoven
60 ——— Installation view
Van Abbemuseum, Eindhoven
62 ——— Installation view
Van Abbemuseum, Eindhoven
64 ——— YARD (1961/2007)
Van Abbemuseum, Eindhoven
66 ——— HOUSEHOLD (1964/2006)
Kieswerk Mächler, Munich
October 28, 2006
68 ——— OUT (1964/2006)
Haus der Kunst, Munich
October 17, 2006

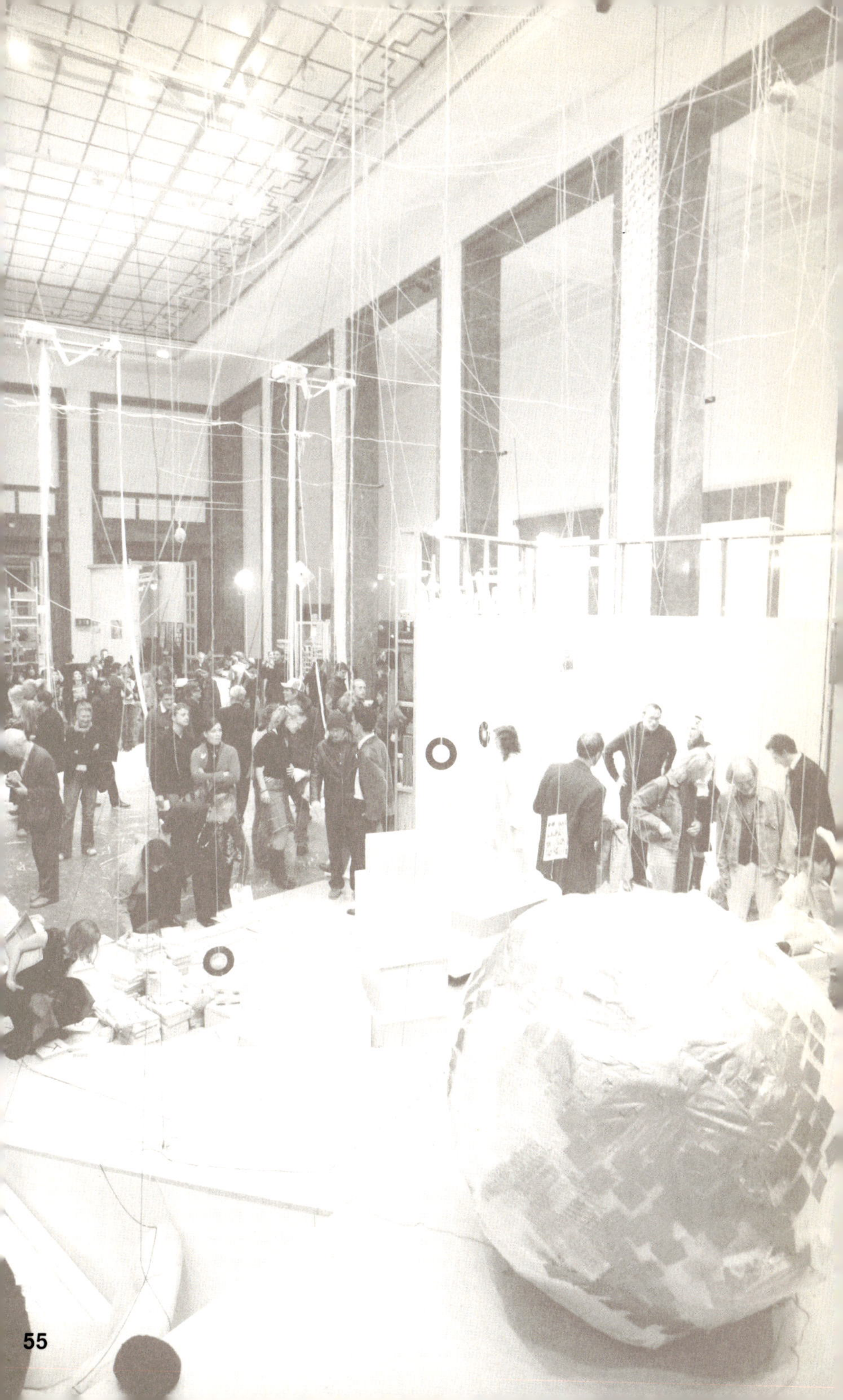

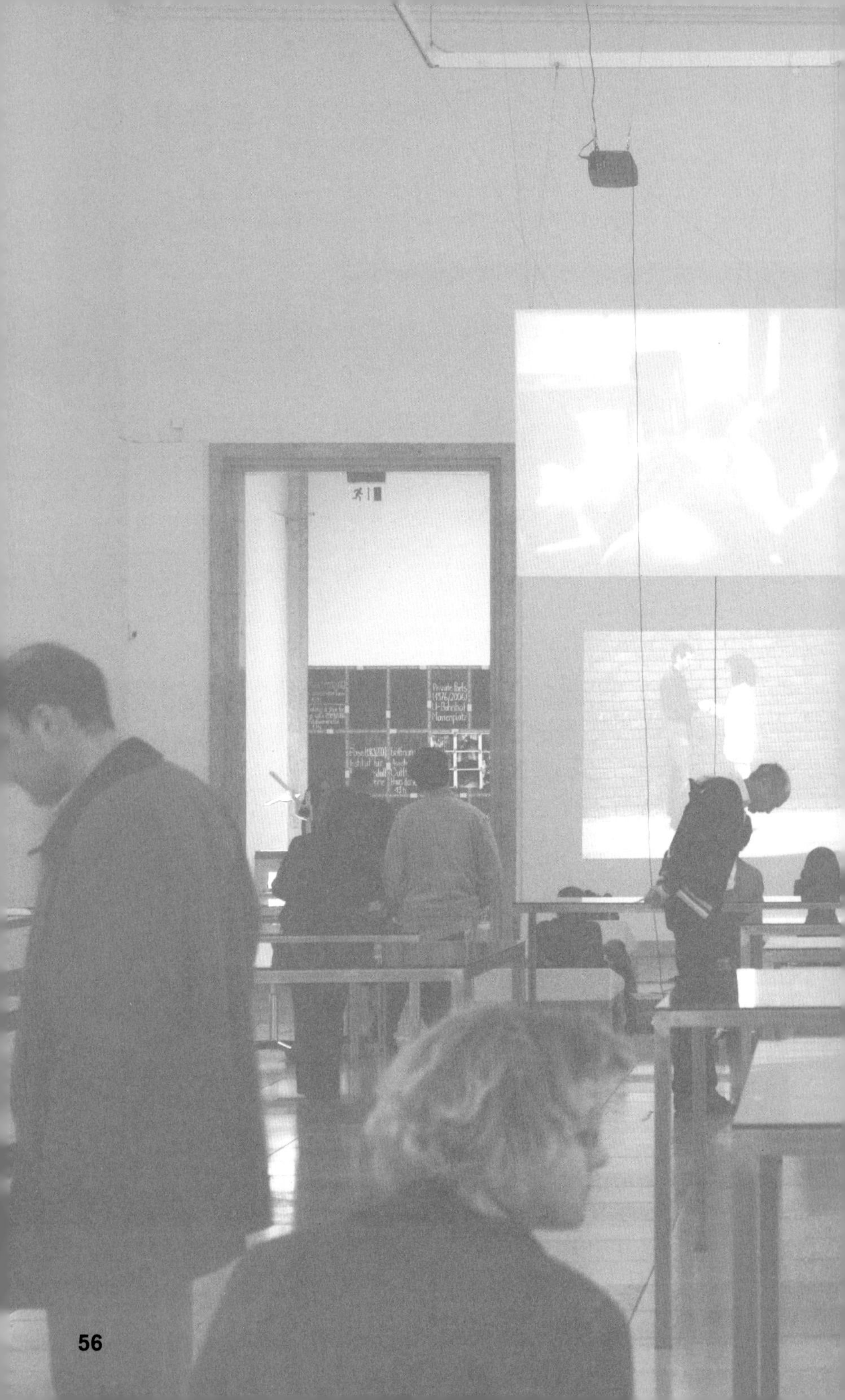
Private Parts
(1976/2006)
U-Bahnhof

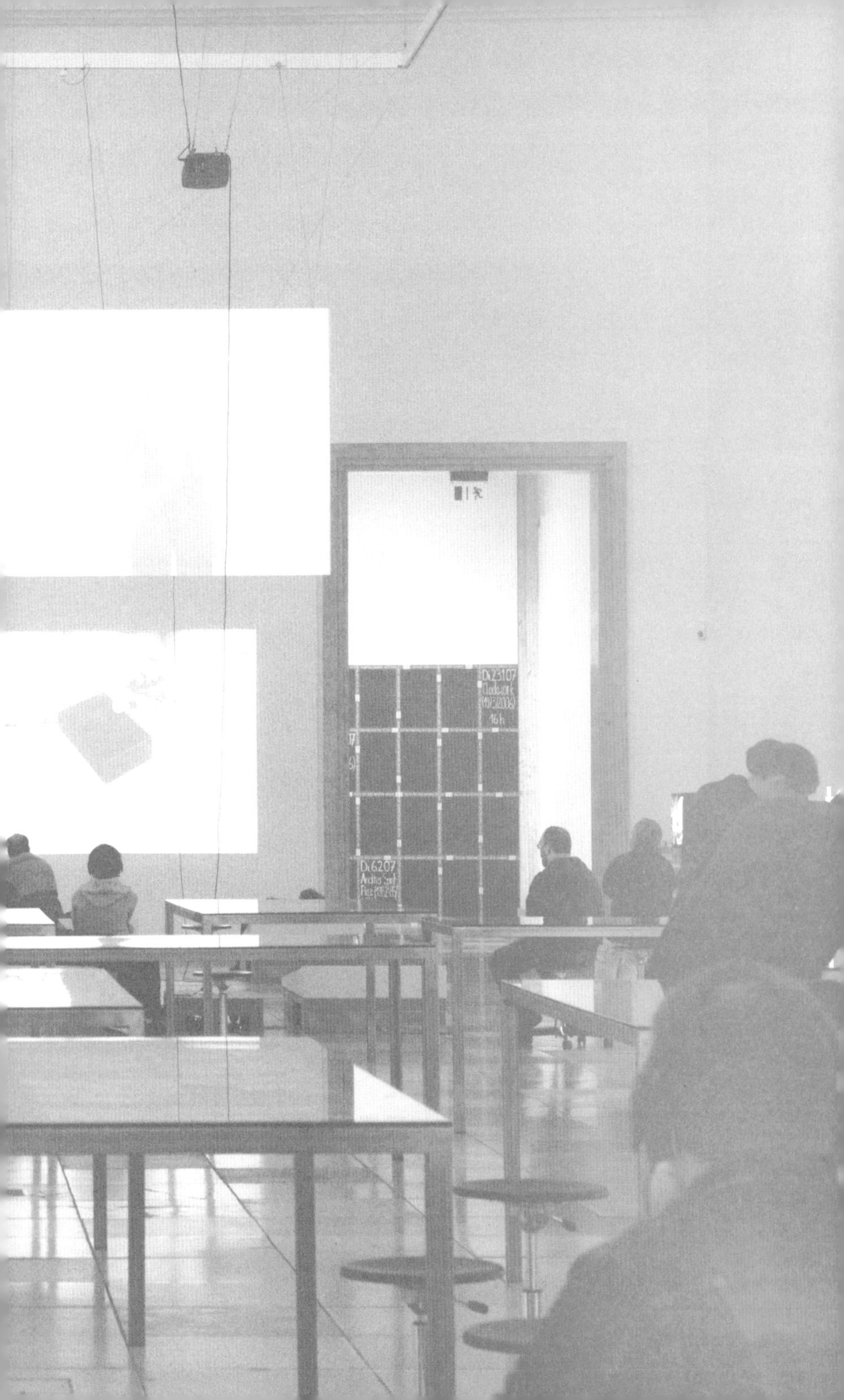

Di.23.1.07
16 h
Di.6.2.07

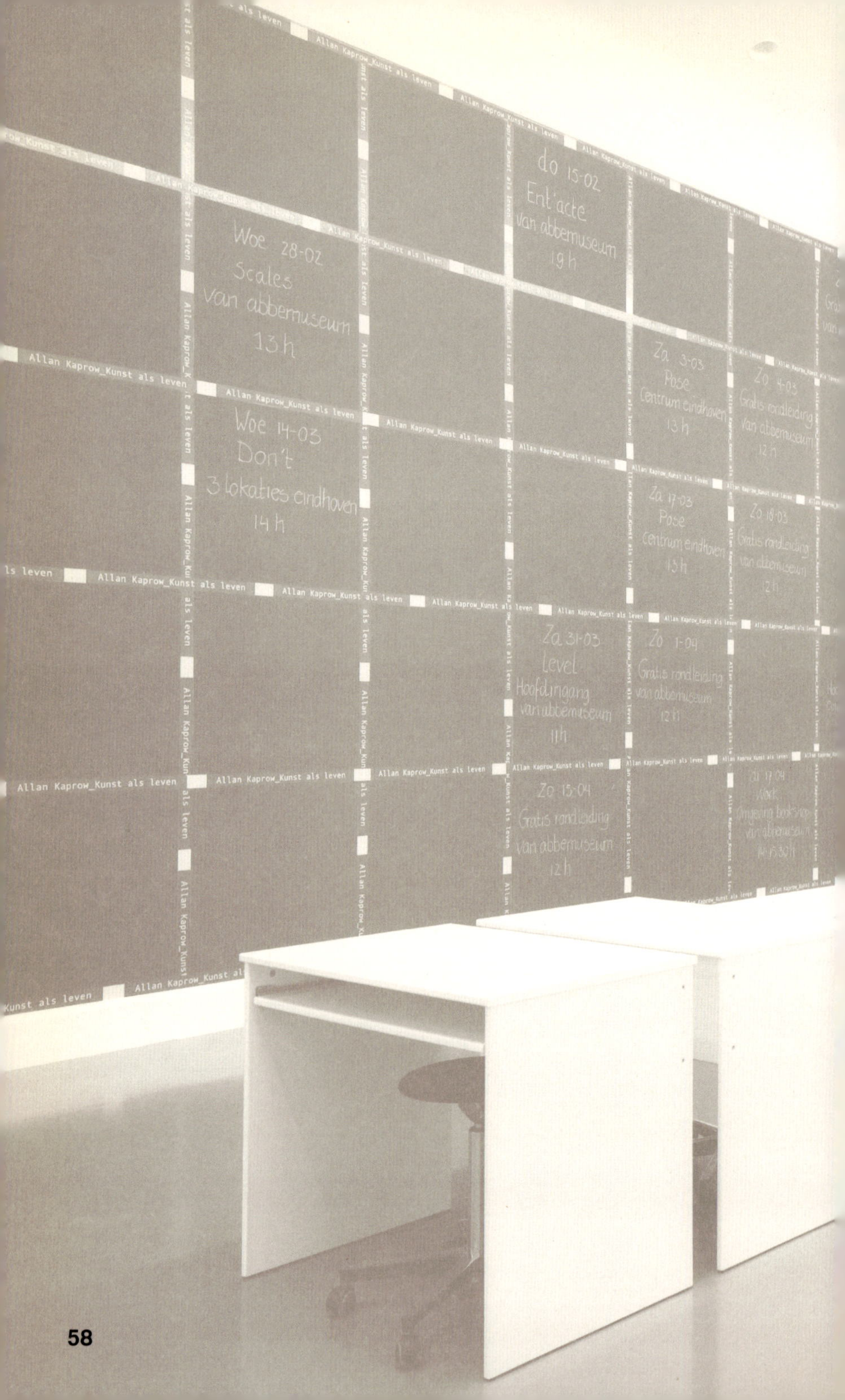
Allan Kaprow_Kunst als leven
do 15-02
Ent'acte
van abbemuseum
19 h
Woe 28-02
Scales
van abbemuseum
13 h
Za 3-03
Pose
Centrum eindhoven
13 h
Zo 4-03
Gratis rondleiding
van abbemuseum
12 h
Woe 14-03
Don't
3 lokaties eindhoven
14 h
Za 17-03
Pose
Centrum eindhoven
13 h
Zo 18-03
Gratis rondleiding
van abbemuseum
12 h
Za 31-03
Level
Hoofdingang
van abbemuseum
11 h
Zo 1-04
Gratis rondleiding
van abbemuseum
12 h
Zo 15-04
Gratis rondleiding
van abbemuseum
12 h

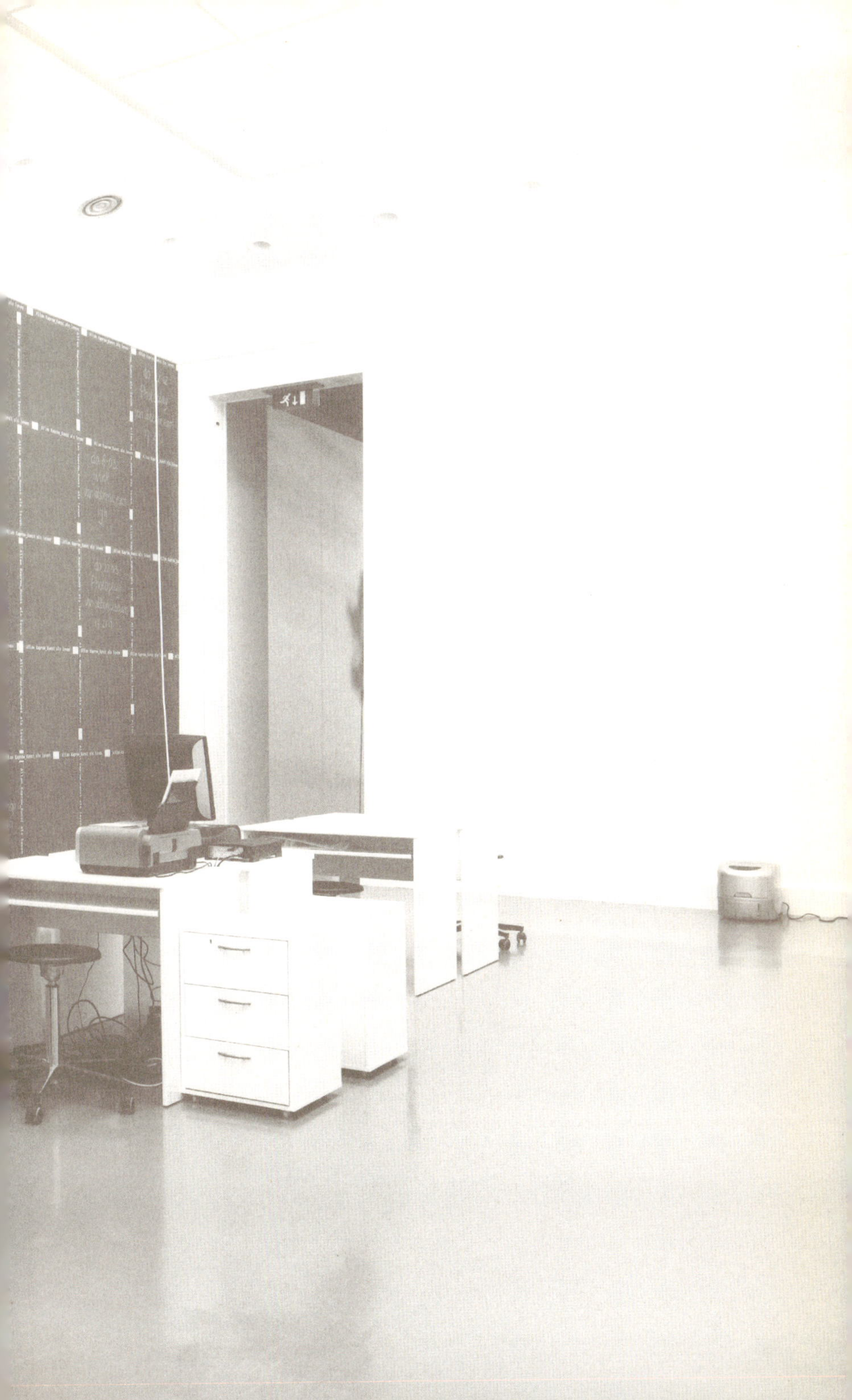

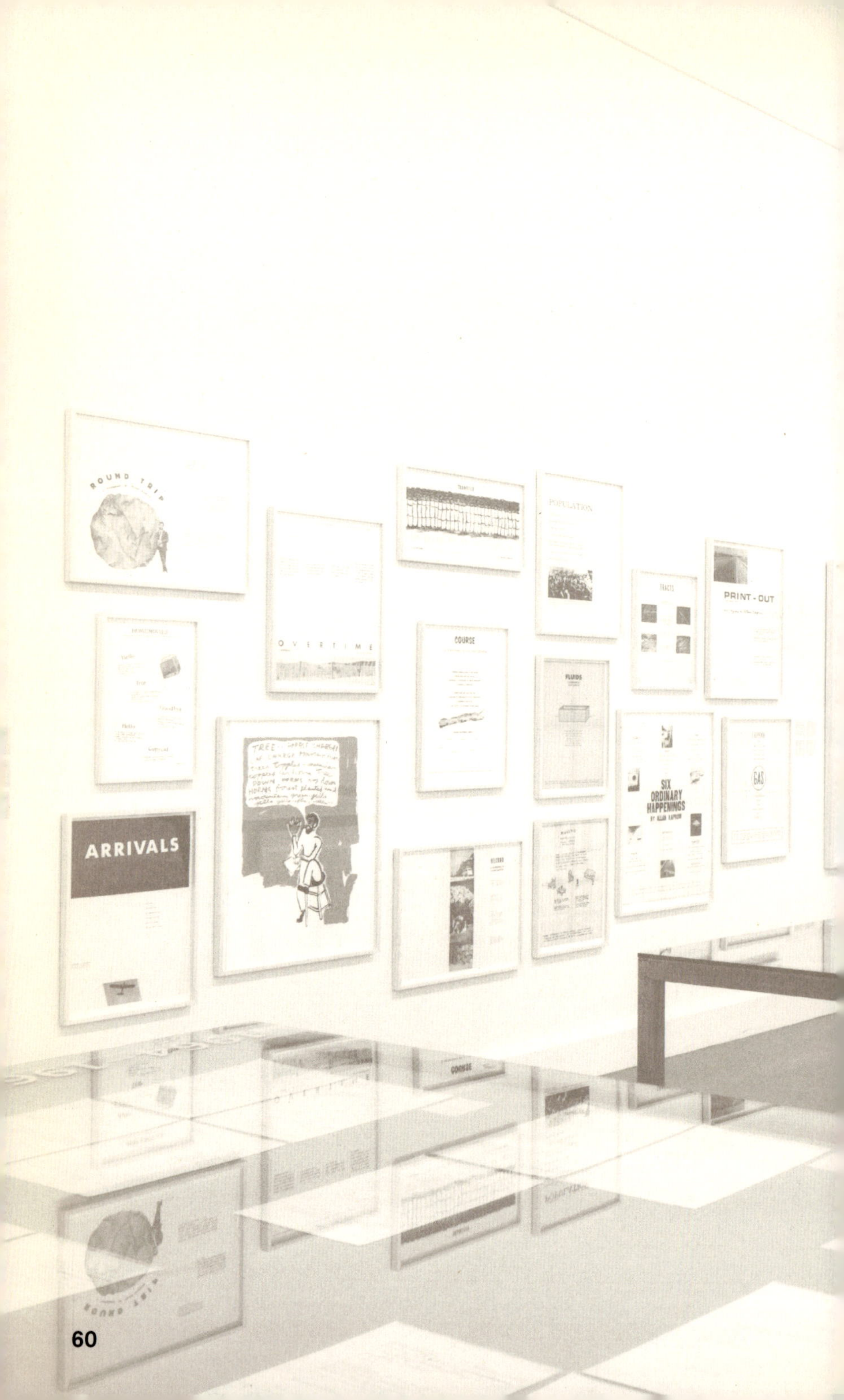
ROUND TRIP
OVERTIME
POPULATION
PRINT - OUT
COURSE
ARRIVALS
SIX ORDINARY HAPPENINGS BY ALLAN KAPROW
GAS

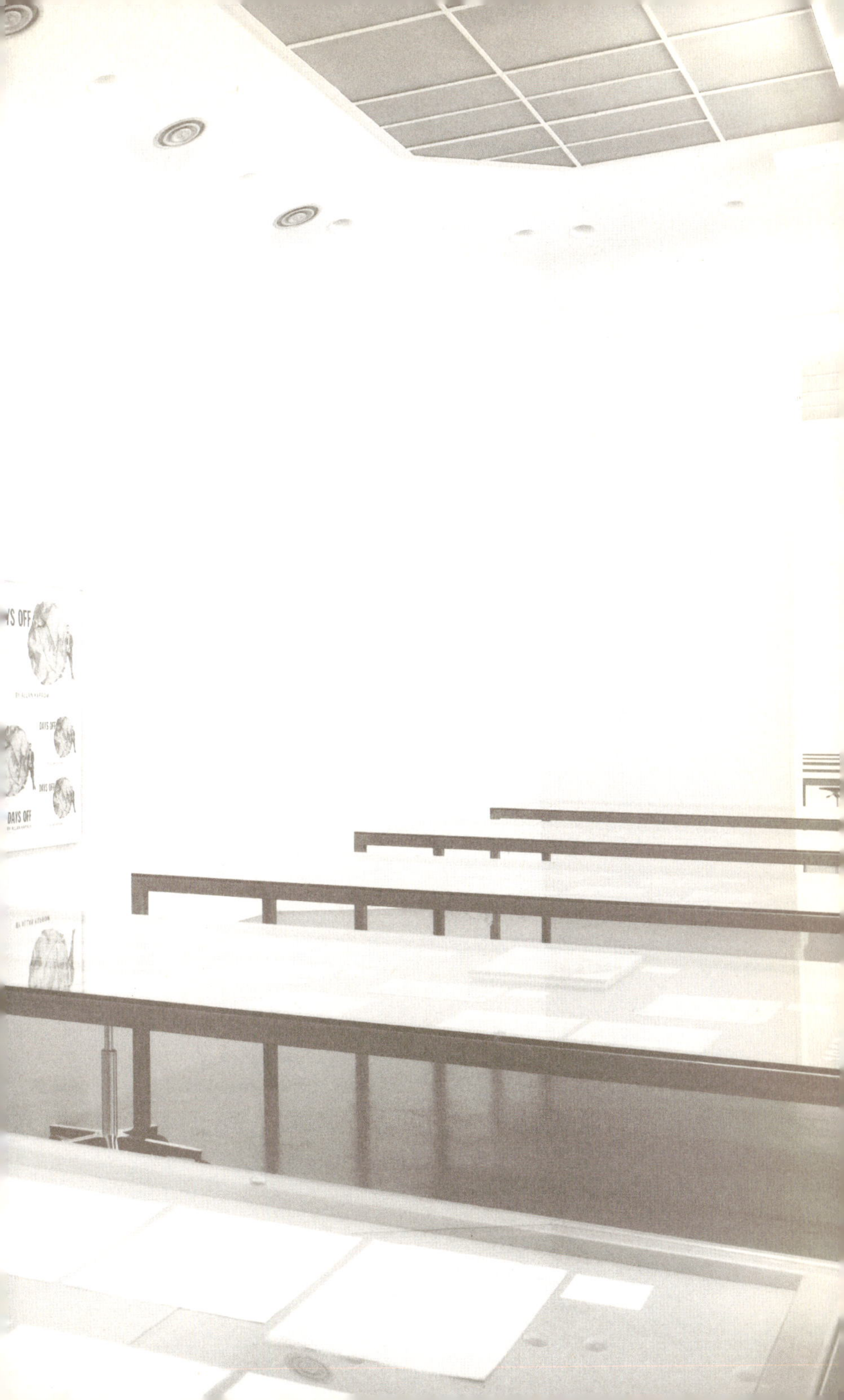
DAYS OFF
DAYS OFF
DAYS OFF

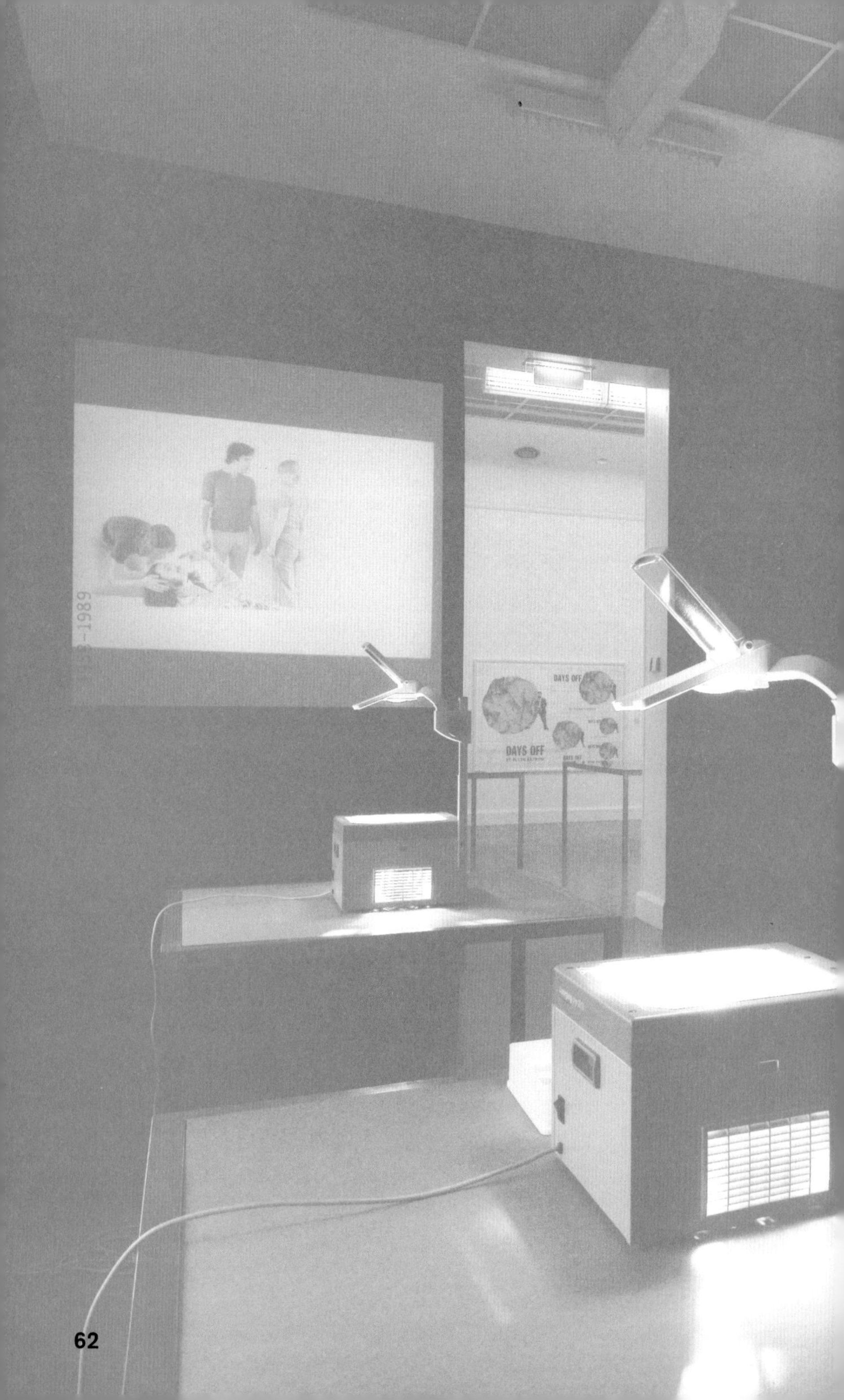
DAYS OFF
DAYS OFF

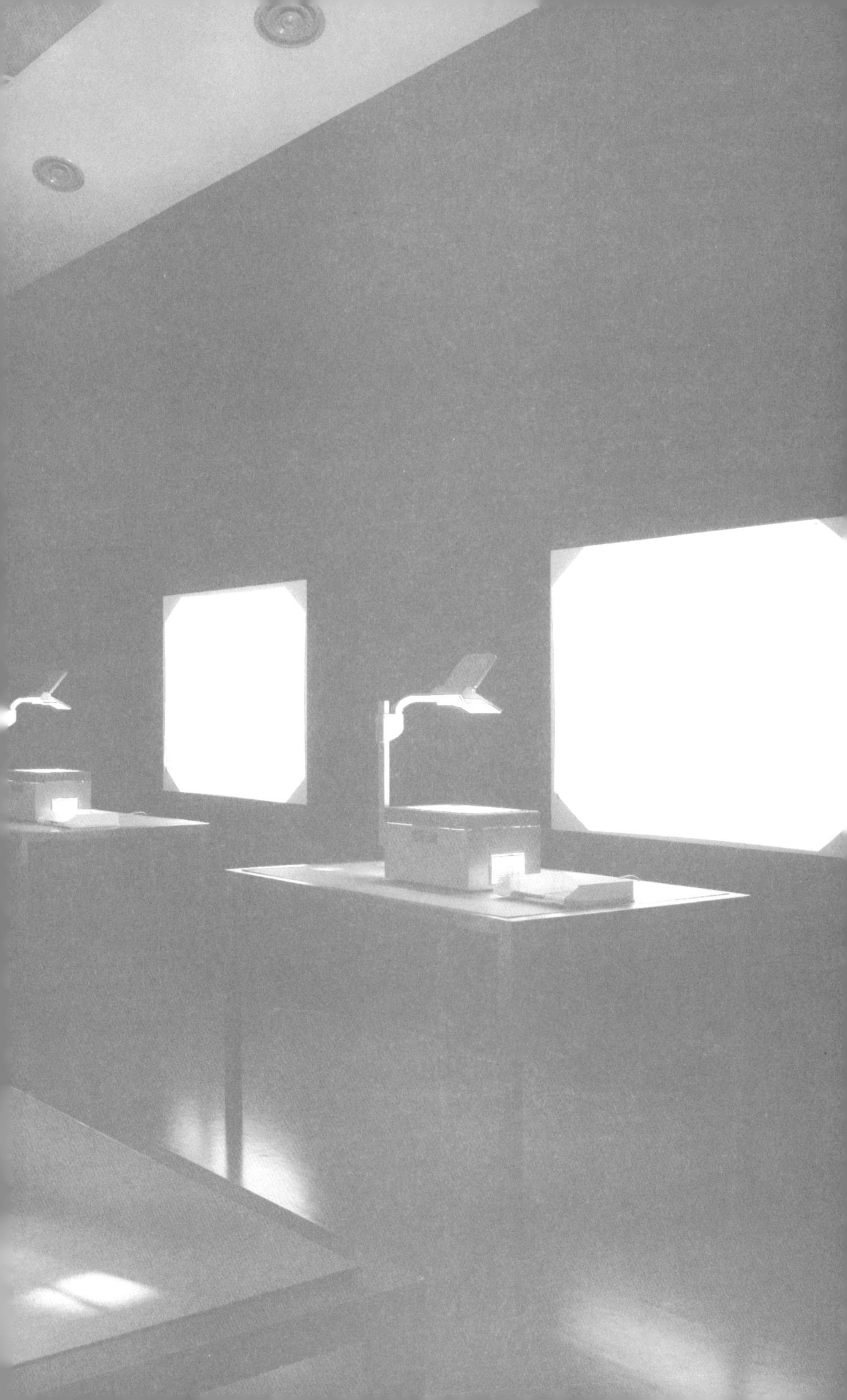

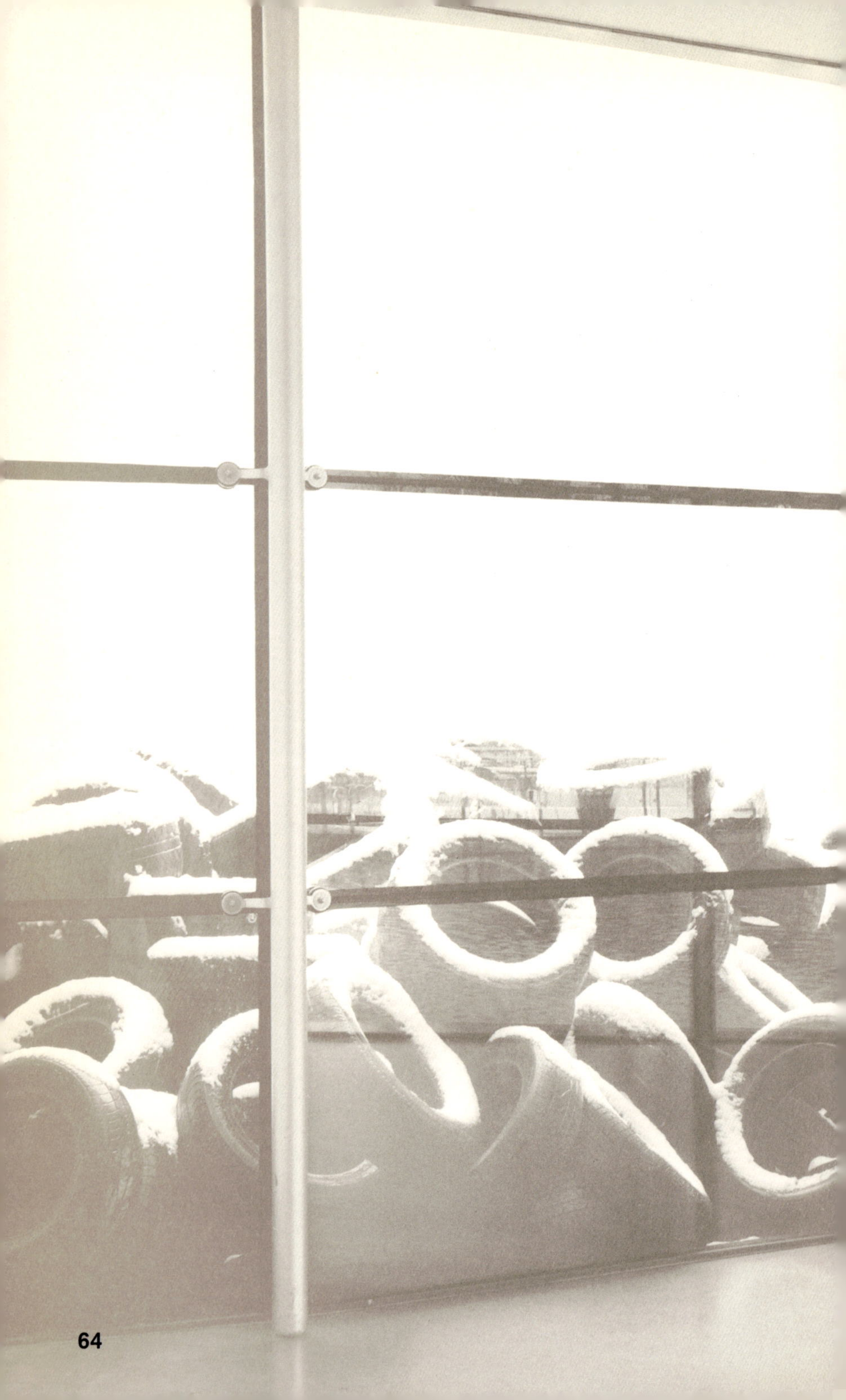

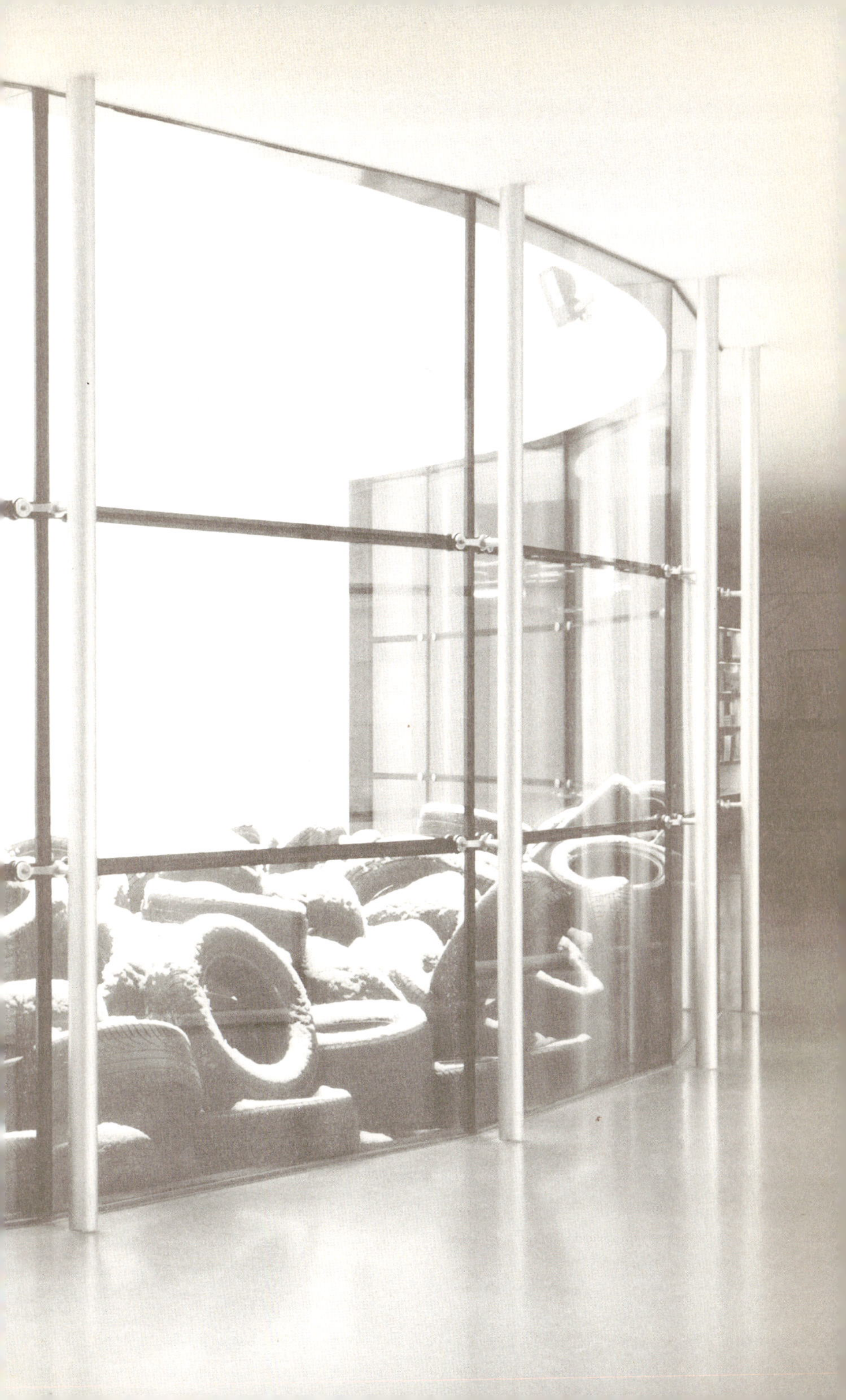

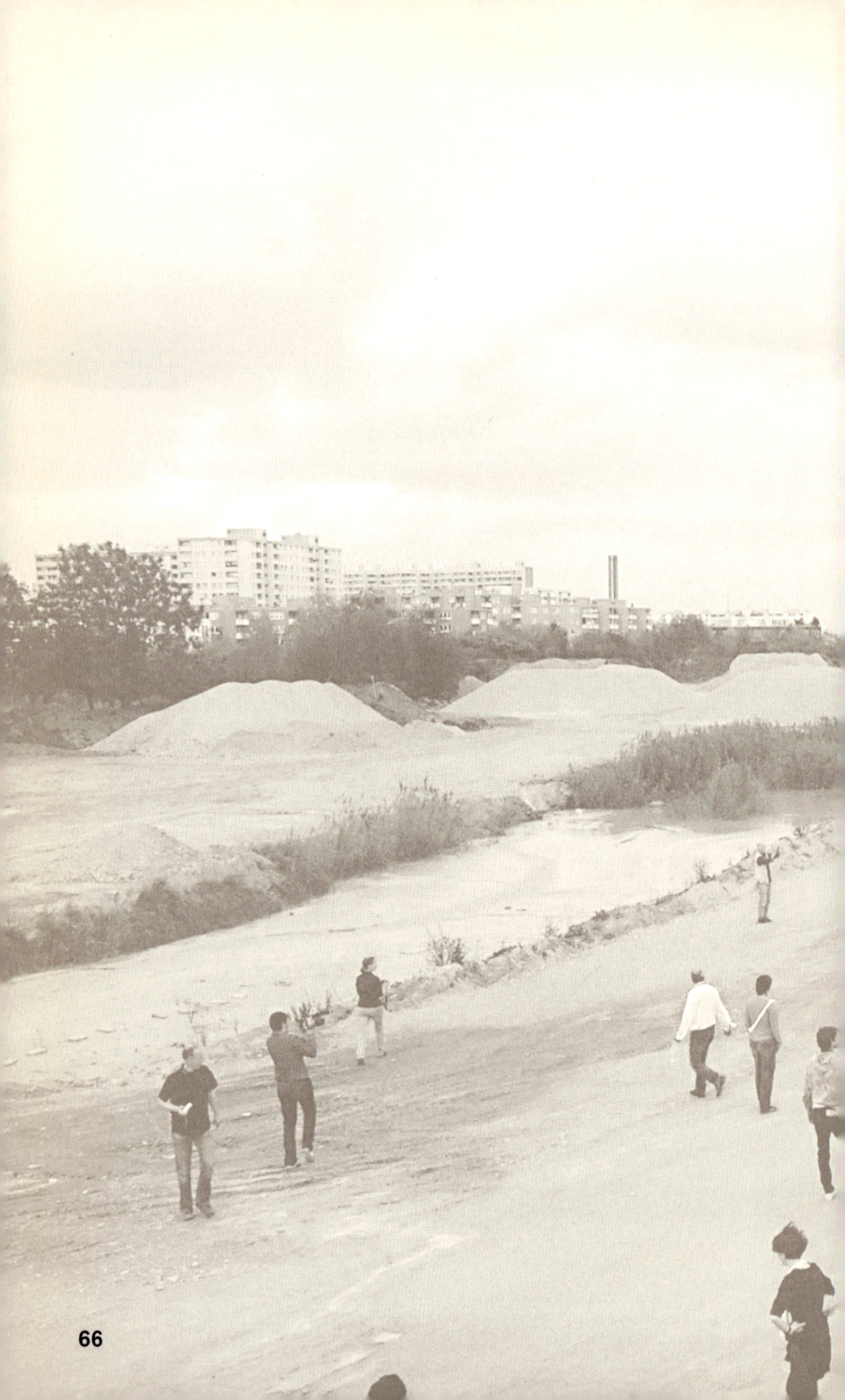

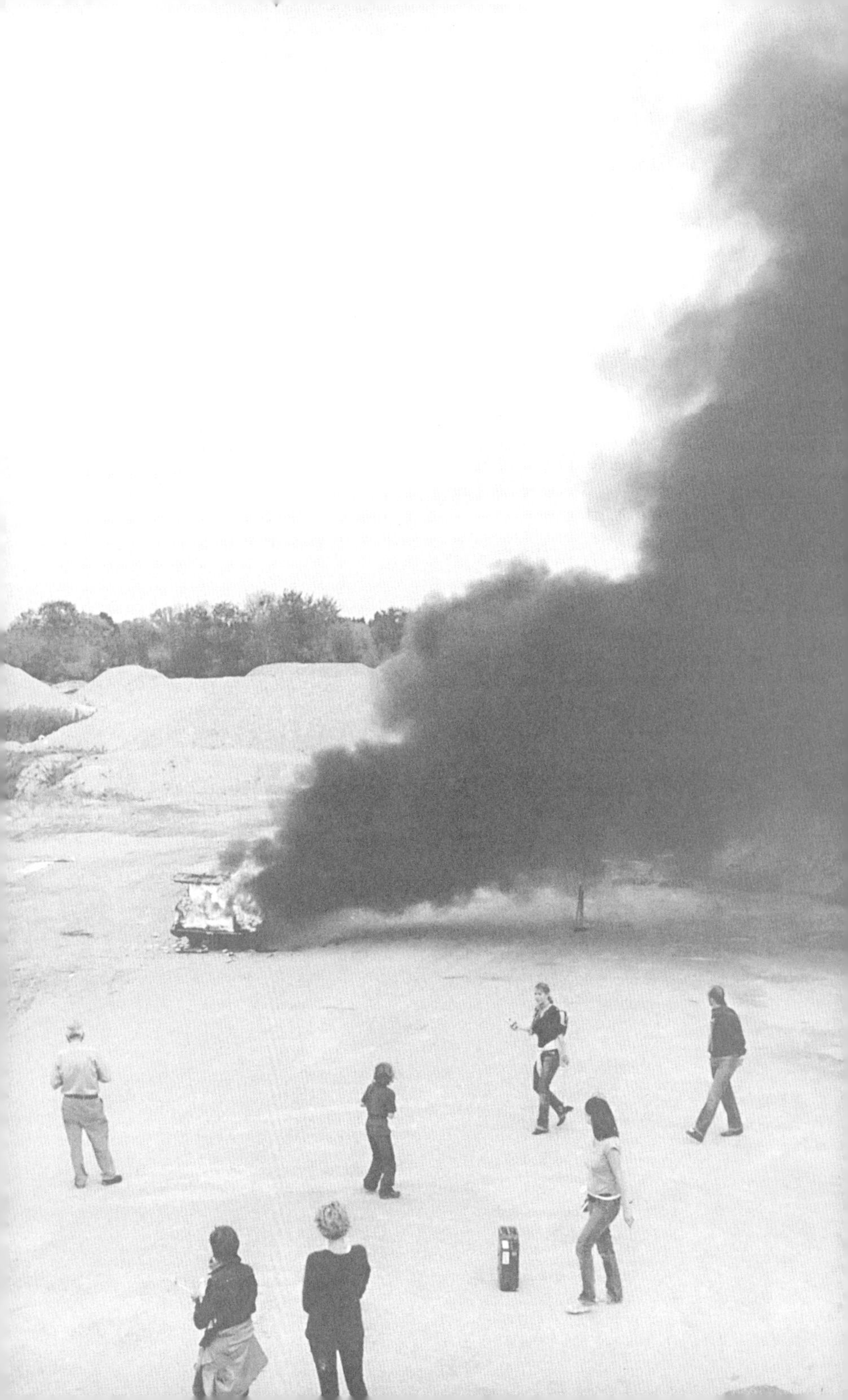

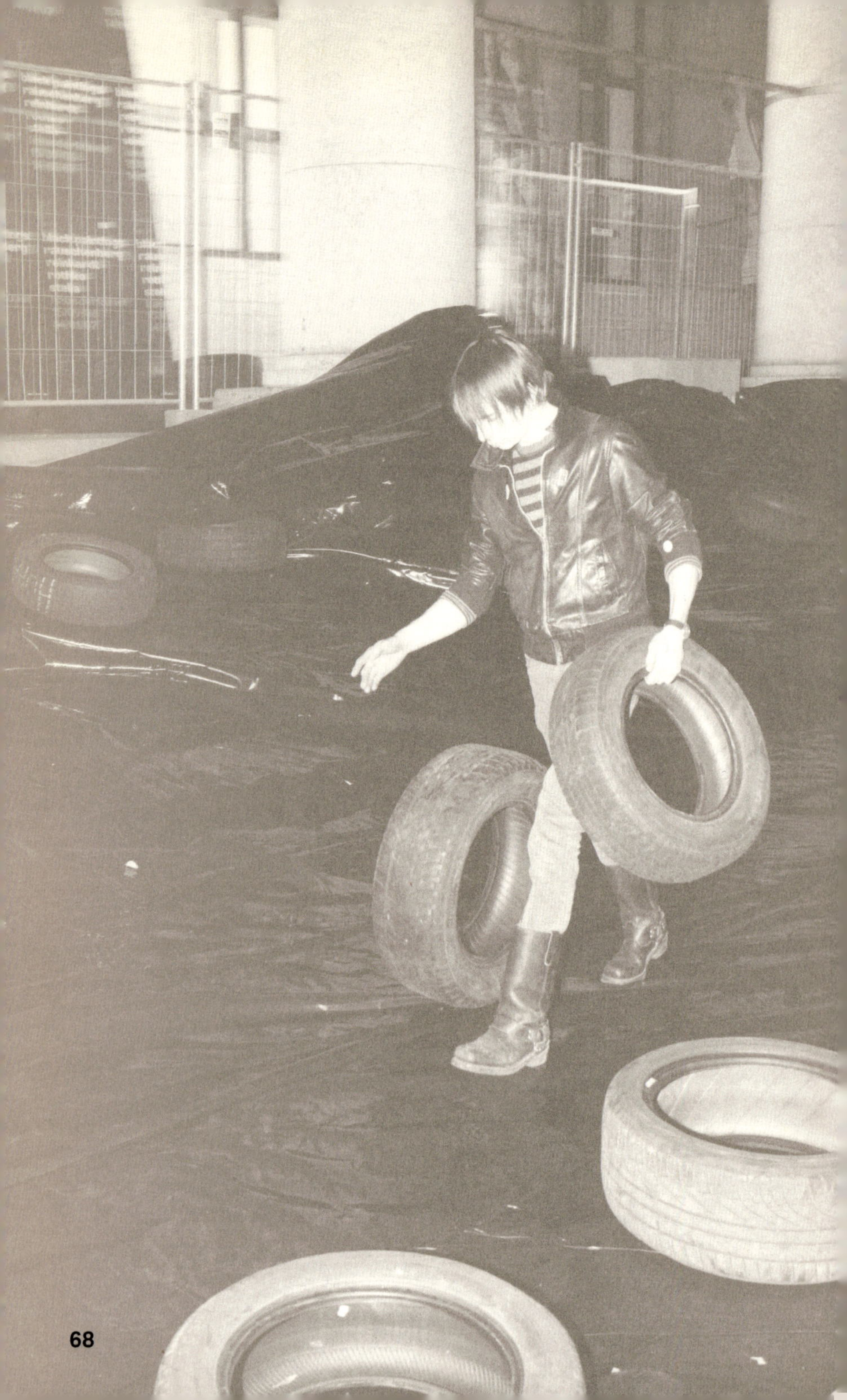

MUSEUM AS MEDIATION

Eva Meyer-Hermann

——— Anyone arriving at the Van Abbemuseum in Eindhoven during the exhibition *Allan Kaprow. Kunst als leven / Art as Life* had the choice of three entrances. None of these was more important than the others; the visitor's first sight of the exhibition was thus deliberately left to chance. To the right the visitor was confronted by the figurative paintings of Kaprow's early years, straight ahead projections of photographs lit up the walls. To the left was a room with a large array of handyman's tools, apparently just waiting to be used. In addition to that, there were large-format video projections of people engaged in strange acts of communication and performing outlandish behavioral rituals.

——— Each of the three points of access to the work of Allan Kaprow led into very different materials and media. The paintings and collages fulfilled the public's customary expectations of art and of a classic museum presentation. Viewers found themselves face to face with the works, and could identify, for instance, with the figure in a domestic scene or an urban situation; even the abstract collages seemed to reflect the material world of their own (daily) lives. The image and the viewer each had their own zone; the connection between the two was linear and reflexive. However, the enclosed nature of the presentation of Kaprow's early work was disrupted by a huge, free-standing screen with a flickering projection of a film of the early Happening *Household* (1964). In some remote, inhospitable terrain groups of men and women are seen constructing nests and towers, only to destroy them again; the activity seems to be based on some kind of a battle of the sexes. The viewer could also relate to the moving pictures which underlined the fact that, for Kaprow, painting as representation had reached its limits and that its symbolic function was being taken over by the Activities he began to devise in the 1960s.

——— The projected photographs at the second entrance presented a different embodiment of reality. As a rule photography is credited with containing a high level of reality. There is a widespread belief that the paper with its chemical emulsion depicts exactly what once was. However, in this room the photographs were not presented as self-explanatory, authentic evidence, and only came into sight following the viewer's intervention, in the sense that the visual material existed only in the form of acetates that the exhibition visitor could choose and place on the overhead projectors. The viewer thus became an author of sorts, or at least an editor, and certainly an agent, putting together visuals for themselves and others. And since each person could fulfill their role as agent as they thought fit, the information lost its apparent exclusivity, its supposed authority. Instead of a vis-à-vis involving the viewer and the image, the exhibition visitor became involved in a constantly shifting relationship.

———And, by the same token, there was no "authentic" arrangement of the accumulation of materials and objects inside the third entrance. Earlier visitors had obviously already left their mark here and the open nature of the configuration of items invited subsequent visitors to do the same. The work itself was a free reinvention of the large-scale Environment *Stockroom*, first realized by Kaprow in 1961. There was no artistic outcome or end point as such; what counted was the process of constant change. Around the walls there were videos of other Happenings and Activities. These films were not intended to be regarded as works of art in their own right; they were simply yet another medium giving the visitor access to Kaprow's "extended" concept of artistic work.

———So, did the first entrance literally give the visitor a picture of his art? And was the next using photographic reproductions to pin down the historical facts? Or does one have the keenest sense of Kaprow's work, as at the third entrance, when one plunges into the almost overwhelming mass of materials and possibilities and starts to actively engage with their physical, psychological, social, and other mechanisms? The point of these three entrances was to show that all these questions and statements could be both right and wrong, that they are all open to contradiction, that there is no single, right way. All his life Kaprow was highly critical of museums. In the 1960s he decried them as mausoleums and proposed that they should be left unoccupied, or turned into night clubs or swimming pools. But he did also constantly try to come up with constructive suggestions as to how museums or the public school system could fittingly be used to mediate art.

———In our discussions concerning the upcoming exhibitions in Munich and Eindhoven, Stephanie Rosenthal and I repeatedly returned to the question of how we could devise a suitable presentation form in view of the historical importance of Kaprow's work, the unanswerable questions that were intrinsic to it, the vast amount of material, and, not least, the artist's own unrelenting critical scrutiny of all we were doing. In a nutshell, the question was: can and should this work be exhibited at all? And what would "exhibition" mean in these circumstances, even if the word were to be replaced by Kaprow's preferred alternative, namely "presentation"? And didn't this project embody the very question that most museums have sought to avoid since the 1960s, that is to say, are museums even in a position to exhibit something that has always staunchly resisted them and the idea of exhibiting things? Had Allan Kaprow's art—in keeping with its declared intention—migrated into daily life; had it really completely turned its back on the museum; more than that, was it lost to the museum forever? Or might it be possible, necessary even, to "capture" something of this ephemeral art of interconnections in an art institution, to present one of its aggregate states within the walls of a museum, thereby confirming that the art museum can also play a part in daily life?

——— In response to a statement by the artist, we came up with two guiding principles for our exhibition concept: "Museum as Mediation" and "Agency for Action." In the same way that Kaprow wanted to educate "uneducated" non-artists, our paradoxical aim was to organize a "non-exhibition." In keeping with the artist's hopes for his own work, visitors to the exhibition were not to be mere spectators, or worse still, consumers, but were to actively participate in it. Kaprow's radical concept of art that was both entirely site-specific and ephemeral was to be reflected in the focus on the transient nature of the exhibition, which would take on a different aspect in each location. Instead of presenting fixed interpretations, our goal was to make the viewer an open offer on the basis of existing documents.

——— The majority of the materials on display were Kaprow's so-called scores. Following the principle of the "Museum as Mediation," over 300 of these sheets were presented in chronological order in a long sequence of flat display cases. There was no additional visual information explaining the individual sheets: that would of necessity have cast the display as a historical reconstruction. The scores were presented as a "genre" in their own right, as one of the aggregate states of the work. No limits were put on the viewer's powers of imagination, memory, and fantasy as they read the typed and handwritten texts and instructions for an almost endless series of Happenings and Activities. The idea was not to illustrate Kaprow's ideas and projects but to unleash and to disseminate the creativity still stored within them.

——— The scores were the primary source of inspiration for the overarching exhibition principle of the "Museum as Mediation." What happens if visitor-participants are presented with the materials arranged according to genres and media, such that any predetermined integration or interpretation is deliberately avoided? What coincidences, associations, personal circumstances, and knowledge will then shape the viewers' picture of Kaprow's art? It was as though the non-hierarchically structured exhibition "composed" itself with the aid of the visitor-participants—in the best-case scenario as in a musical group improvisation. The museum as the provider of authoritative interpretations remained very much in the background. It served simply as a "mediation tool" where materials were laid out to be examined and even handled.

——— Meanwhile the principle of the "Agency for Action" was the motor powering the exhibition. If the organizers were not able to turn the exhibition visitors into participants by engaging them in Activities, the visitors would also not understand the different sections and the materials on offer as instructions. The Environments—first realized between 1958 and 1964—that were reinvented for the exhibitions played an important part in the "activation" of the visitors. As with the Happenings and Activities, Kaprow had delegated responsibility for the reinventions of the Environments to the curators, having previously always retained control himself. The full significance of the fact that third parties can now realize pieces by Kaprow is impossible to estimate as yet, for it opens up a whole new range of responses to his work.

——— In Eindhoven the Environments served as a means to eradicate the dividing line between visitors and the art that is traditionally established by the exhibition process. The four Environments realized for the Eindhoven exhibition were conceived with the guidance and "activation" of the visitor in mind and, hence, developed by the curator in situ. *Words* used collages of historic text fragments (in the form of digitally stored agglomerations) in combination with the spontaneous utterances of visitors to explore the limits of language. *Push & Pull* played with the principle of superimposed compositional elements both in the form of a document and as an activity, while *Stockroom* divested artistic activity of its usual halo and pared it back to a more general sense of "making." *Yard* was a poetic landscape created from perfectly ordinary car tires and invited visitors to indulge in a somewhat whimsical bodily experience.

——— Thus the exhibition aspired to map out a new path somewhere between traditional museum presentations of objects and relics on one hand, that so often end up as fetishes, and, on the other hand, the problematic suggestivity of a documentary reconstruction. It offered viewers a multiplicity of different elements with which to approach Kaprow's artistic activity which was, by definition, non-hierarchical and ephemeral. The different sections all drew on the tangible evidence of Kaprow's art, but the overriding aim was the intangible outcome of his Activities that it initiated and should continue to instigate.

Eva Meyer-Hermann is a free-lanced Exhibitions maker, based in Cologne, formerly Senior Curator at the Van Abbemuseum, Eindhoven.

Translated from the German by **Fiona Elliott**

THE RISK OF WELCOMING THE PUBLIC

Stephanie Rosenthal

Is there ever any hope of devising a fitting presentation mode in public institutions for art forms that specifically resist the notion of art works as exhibits? This was the question facing Eva Meyer-Hermann and myself in 2004 when we decided to realize an exhibition of the work of the American artist Allan Kaprow. I was in a paradoxical situation: I was going to Encinitas, California, in the hope of creating an exhibition with an artist who particularly interested me because he had always refused to put on exhibitions, had never become part of the art market, and had only ever used his art to get a better hold on his own life. All of these factors ought to have meant it would not be possible to create an exhibition with Allan Kaprow. And yet I was convinced that precisely his art could potentially be the focus of a very special form of exhibition: an exhibition that would involve the public in a way that had not been tried hitherto; an exhibition that would give the visitor a chance to reassess certain daily processes through the filter of Kaprow's work and, hence, through art itself.

——— All his life Allan Kaprow had an ambivalent attitude to exhibitions. He showed no interest either in his works being exhibited in art museums or in a classical retrospective. "Eventually…the modern museum may gradually lose that cloying association of holiness that it presently inherits from another age. Hopefully, it will become an educational institute, a computerized bank of cultural history, and an agency for action." (Kaprow 1967) When Eva Meyer-Hermann and I first met him to discuss our exhibition project, Kaprow's opening words were, "Here's the problem: I don't want to have a show!" [1] This statement was wholly at odds with the fact that he had specifically invited us to visit him. From that point onward our discussions continued on the basis of the realization that Kaprow's resistance was deeply rooted in his artistic outlook. In the end he agreed that the exhibition should go ahead, on condition that his art wouldn't end up in a graveyard, and bade us farewell with the words, "I have to take a risk. I have to trust the public." So the challenge now facing us was to turn the Haus der Kunst into an "Agency for Action".

——— Accordingly the focus of the exhibition was not on the early collages and paintings but on the transient, performative side of Kaprow's work. We decided to divide the exhibition into two sections: "Museum as Mediation" and "Agency for Action." In the Haus der Kunst the physical and conceptual transition between these two realms was the Central Hall, which became a conduit to the "classical" exhibition rooms in the East Wing. On display here were new versions of the Environments *Stockroom* (1961), *Words* (1962), and *Push and Pull* (1963), realized by students from the classes of three professors at Munich University,

---

1 Allan Kaprow in conversation with the curators, 14 December 2004, Encinitas, California.

Magdalena Jetelová, Hermann Pitz, and Stefan Römer. Since Kaprow's Environments are not classical installations but rooms to be filled, exhibition visitors were invited to participate in the works, to interact with the specially created space, and to consciously see themselves as elements in the composition of the Environments. As a result, the Environments were constantly changing.

——— "Museum as Mediation" was the zone in which we presented scores, Activity Booklets and notes by the artist in display cases, audio and visual materials, and documentary photographs shown on overhead projectors. The aim was not to present a strictly documentary account of the Happenings, since we felt it was more appropriate to present the individual media separately so that any overview would only exist in the viewer's mind. In our minds this zone was central to the exhibition, for it illuminated the sheer variety of Kaprow's output. Kaprow's poetic, comic, simple, complex, scurrilous, imaginative scores amply rewarded visitors who were able to engage with them on a deeper level.

——— "Agency for Action" referred to the re-invented Happenings, and thus to the part of the exhibition that was not visible, hard to grasp and yet crucial to the exhibition as a whole. During that first visit Kaprow already mentioned that he had been thinking about delegating responsibility for his Happenings to others. Since Kaprow's Happenings and Activities were about participation, it seemed logical to allow new versions to be made by other people rather than keeping the Happenings on such a short personal rein that they would, by definition, cease to exist when his own life ended. So he decided, for the purposes of this exhibition, to invite others to realize new versions of his Happenings, in effect to "re-invent" them. In so doing he was separating his art from his life—the two having been inextricably intertwined hitherto. He was also remaining true to the principle he had established in the early 1960s, namely that Happenings could not be repeated, for the new versions were not to be replicas of his own versions, but were to be different. This new venture was a radical step on Kaprow's part and it has given his output an entirely new dimension. We, as curators, therefore decided that the exhibition should reflect this change and that its making should embody the principles that Kaprow himself laid down for any re-inventions of his Happenings: "site-specificity," "impermanence," and "doubt in art."

——— Although Kaprow was relinquishing his own personal control, he was delegating control to another individual. This was the logical outcome of his own experience that control creates freedom. With his scores he had provided guidelines, a point of reference that can either serve as a springboard or can be left to one side. The re-invented version would be entirely dependent on the Leader, the time, the place, and the participants. This part of the exhibition presented me with a

———

2 Ibid.

very considerable challenge, since there was a danger that it could turn Kaprow's art into a playground or reduce it to a "find-yourself" experience. And then there was also the question as to whether it was still relevant—in the early twenty-first century—to realize Happenings, some of which Kaprow had enacted in the late 1950s. It should not be forgotten that Kaprow himself continued to put on Happenings right up until 2003. And yet I knew that I would only be able to answer this question to my own satisfaction if I were to participate in any Happenings myself. In addition to this, a high degree of openness would be required of all the participants. We were all well aware that communication and a willingness to arrive at joint decisions were crucial to Kaprow's works. To formulate this requirement in theoretical terms is one thing, to put it into practice is another. It would have been easy and rather more effective to take certain decisions regarding the Happenings ourselves, but we had decided to engage in a collective process. So the opening of the exhibition was preceded by a period of talks, discussions, and a process of joint decision-making. In Munich more than twenty-five Happenings were re-invented in public spaces, in other institutions, and in the Haus der Kunst itself. For me, what I gained above all from this exhibition was the experience of the world that I entered through the Happenings. Generally it was the things that occurred during the Happenings that no-one could have predicted—that were not in the scores—that left the deepest impressions.

——— For the Munich exhibition we re-invented Kaprow's Happening *Round Trip* (1968). Having spent two hours gathering litter from the street and rolling it into a ball, we were then faced with the task of getting rid of it somehow. Unexpectedly the decision was taken out of our hands by a friendly caretaker who flung the ball into "his" rubbish bin. This Happening thus prompted the participants to think about decision-making processes and responsibility, about one's responsibility as an individual but also as a member of a group. Innumerable questions arose from this—about the role of chance, about the seriousness with which we had been participating in this Action, and about the conclusions that we would draw from these experiences.

——— Within a relatively short space of time in the 1960s Kaprow's œuvre took a new direction. The precisely choreographed and rehearsed key work *18 Happenings in 6 Parts* soon gave way to a radically free artistic form in which the individual participant is crucially entrusted to take responsibility for his/her own actions and experience.

——— What fascinated me about Kaprow's decision to open up his work and to allow others to embark on re-inventions was not only its radicalism but also the fact that he did not hide the pain and effort it cost him. It was impossible for him to think about the possibility of new versions without also having to face his own mortality. In that sense, we became part of a gradual process of separation. Sooner or later exhibition-makers would have started to unearth photographs from the archives and Kaprow would have had no say in the future presentation of his work. By deciding in favor of re-inventions, he had once again taken control and was steering his work in a direction that could be sustained even in his absence. At our first meeting Kaprow had asked, "Can I continue to welcome the public in my world?" With this exhibition he in effect replied "yes" to his own question.

Stephanie Rosenthal is Curator, Haus der Kunst, Munich

Translated from the German by **Fiona Elliott**

——— Allan Kaprow was born in Atlantic City, New Jersey, in 1927. Much of his childhood was spent in Tucson, Arizona, but he returned to New York City to graduate from the High School of Music and Art in 1945. In 1949 he received his BA from New York University, and for the next year worked toward a graduate degree in philosophy. In 1947–48, he also studied painting with Hans Hofmann. He shifted to the study of art history at Columbia University and received his Master's degree in 1952 under Meyer Schapiro. Later, in 1957–58, he studied music composition with John Cage at the New School for Social Research.

——— In 1952 he was a co-founder of the historic Hansa Gallery in New York and he exhibited regularly throughout the 1950s. Since then, Kaprow's work has been shown extensively throughout the United States and Europe. He has had more than 30 one-person exhibitions, including retrospectives, at the Pasadena Art Museum, Pasadena, California, 1967; Kunsthalle Bremen, Bremen, Germany, 1976; Museum am Ostwall, Dortmund, Germany, 1986; University of Texas in Arlington, 1988; Fondazione Mudima, Milan, Italy, 1991; Galerie Donguy, Paris, France, 1992; John Gibson Gallery, New York, 1995; and Galerie Hauser & Wirth, Zürich, Switzerland, 2005.

——— By 1957, Kaprow's work became exclusively environmental, involving lights, electronic sounds, odors, and other unusual materials. In 1958, Kaprow exhibited his first "arrangements" at Hansa Gallery. Containing no art objects as such the art was experienced as a surrounding rather than a picture or sculpture to be looked at—a surrounding which engaged the visitor with things to move, switches to manipulate, obstacles to climb, and food to eat. For the next seven years, he expanded the potential of the "Environment," as it came to be called.

——— Gradually the showcase space was abandoned for more informal and natural settings such as vacant breweries, open fields, beaches and woods. Invitations for Kaprow, and commissions for such works, came from universities in the United States and from art institutions abroad. In the same period of 1957–58, Kaprow developed the "happening" as an extension of the environmental concept; contributing an unexpected concept and household word to our spoken language, in the process; and an art form, Happenings, that in various ways and under different names has been practiced all over the world.

——— In Kaprow's form of Happening, ordinary people, ordinary time and everyday spaces like streets, houses and shops, were frequently merged into ordinary activities such as wallpapering a room, digging ditches or taking a pulse. Fantasy was never absent, but there was always a commitment to shared or common experience. Art and life were blurred. By 1969, Kaprow's work had evolved so distinctly into a new phase that he gave up the designation "Happening" and adopted colleague Michael Kirby's term "Activity."

——— Between 1958 and his death in 2006 Allan Kaprow executed nearly 250 such events. His work has been sponsored by major institutions around the world: the Museum of Modern Art in New York; the Museum of Contemporary Art in Chicago; the Walker Art Center in Minneapolis, Minnesota; the Pasadena Art Museum in California; Cornell University in Ithaca, New York; University of Michigan, Ann Arbor; University of California at Berkeley; Massachusetts Institute of Technology in Cambridge; Musée National d'Art Moderne, Centre Georges Pompidou in Paris, France; Akademie der Künste in Berlin, Germany; Galeria Foksal in Warsaw, Poland; Comune di Milano Ripartizione iniziative culturali, Milan, Italy; Museum des 20. Jahrhunderts (MUMOK) in Vienna, Austria; Biennials in Lyon, France; Leipzig, Germany, and Venice, Italy; and documenta in Kassel, Germany.

——— At the time of his death in April 2006, the artist was working with two curators, Stephanie Rosenthal and Eva Meyer-Hermann on "Art as Life," a creative and innovative presentation of Allan Kaprow's oeuvre, and on the first production since 1959 of his seminal Happening, "18 Happenings in 6 Parts".

Allan Kaprow
18 Happenings in 6 Parts:
9/10/11 November 2006
Haus der Kunst, Munich
8:30 pm

Director
André Lepecki

Choreography /
Assistant Director
Noémie Solomon

Sets and decor
Christin Vahl

Sound design
Shawn Greenlee

Cast of participants
Judith Hummel
Coryl Crane Kaprow
Florian Lauw
Mathilda Legemah
Valerie Masyuta
Serkan Salihoglu
Noémie Solomon
Maximilian Specketer
Jaume Villalba

Two guest painters

Editors
Barry Rosen
Michaela Unterdörfer

Essays
André Lepecki
Eva Meyer-Hermann
Stephanie Rosenthal

Translations
from the German Fiona Elliott
(Meyer-Hermann and Rosenthal)

Copy editor
Michael Mack

Publication coordinators
Sylvia Bandi
Tamara Bloomberg
Michaela Unterdörfer

Photography
Peter Cox
[Page 58, 60, 62, 64, 84]
Marion Vogel
[Page 16, 17, 18, 19, 20, 25, 26, 27,
28, 29, 36, 38, 39, 40,
cover backside]
Marino Solokhov
[Page 15, 21, 22, 23, 24, 30, 31,
32, 33, 34, 35, 37, 41, 42, 43]
Wilfried Petzi
[Page 56, 68]
Andreas Lang
[Page 66]

Graphic design
NORM, Dimitri Bruni &
Manuel Krebs, Zurich

Production and printing
Steidl, Göttingen

Published by
Steidl Hauser & Wirth

ISBN 978-3-86521-488-1
Printed in Germany

Steidl
Düstere Strasse 4
D–37073 Göttingen

www.steidl.de
www.steidlville.com
www.hauserwirth.com